3/10 → 84   3/24 → 100   4/14   96-100
                                      108·119
3/14 → 92   3/31 → 110   4/21   120-144

Enough Rope to Shoot
Yourself in the Foot

Other McGraw-Hill Titles of Interest

Enough Rope to Shoot Yourself in the Foot

Rules for C and C++ Programming

Allen I. Holub

McGraw-Hill

New York San Francisco Washington, D.C. Auckland Bogotá
Caracas Lisbon London Madrid Mexico City Milan
Montreal New Delhi San Juan Singapore
Sydney Tokyo Toronto

McGraw-Hill

A Division of The McGraw-Hill Companies

Library of Congress Cataloging-in-Publication Data

Holub, Allen I.
    Enough rope to shoot yourself in the foot : rules for C & C++
programming / by Allen I. Holub.
        p.   cm.
    Includes index.
    ISBN 0-07-029689-8 (p)
    1. C++ (Computer program language)   2. C(Computer program
language)   I. Title.
QA76.73.C153H625   1995
005.13—dc20   95-35136
                                                        CIP

pb   3 4 5 6 7 8 9 BKP BKP 9 0 0 9 8 7 6

ISBN 0-07-029689-8

*The sponsoring editor of this book was Jennifer Holt DiGiovanna, the
Executive Editor was Robert E. Ostrander; and the book editor, John Baker.*

Printed and bound by Quebecor/Book Press.

McGraw-Hill books are available at special quantity discounts to use as premiums and sales
promotions, or for use in corporate training programs. For more information, please write to
the Director of Special Sales, McGraw-Hill, 11 West 19th Street, New York, NY 10011. Or
contact your local bookstore.

Product or brand names used in this book may be trade names or trademarks. Where we
believe that there may be proprietary claims to such trade names or trademarks, the name
has been used with an initial capital or it has been capitalized in the style used by the name
claimant. Regardless of the capitalization used, all such names have been used in an editorial
manner without any intent to convey endorsement of or other affiliation with the name
claimant. Neither the author nor the publisher intends to express any judgment as to the
validity or legal status of any such proprietary claims.

MH95
0296898

For Amanda

Contents

Acknowledgements

This book was much too long in the making, and I'm indebted to three editors at McGraw-Hill who put up, in succession, with my constant delays: Neil Levine, Dan Gonneau, and Jennifer Holt-DiGiovanna. I'm particularly indebted to Bob DuCharme, who saved me from myself by making a very thorough pass through the initial draft of this book. His suggestions have considerably improved the current volume.

Introduction

The title of this book describes what I consider to be the main problem with both C++ and C: the languages give you so much flexibility that, unless you're willing and able to discipline yourself, you can end up with a large body of unmaintainable gobblygook masquerading as a computer program. You can do virtually anything with these languages, even when you don't want to. This book attempts to get a handle on this problem by presenting a collection of rules of thumb for programming in C and C++ — rules that will hopefully keep you out of trouble to begin with. Though most of the rules given here apply equally to C and C++ programming, I've included a lot of material that is relevant only in the C++ world, concentrated into the final section whenever possible. If you're programming in C only, just ignore the C++ stuff that found its way into earlier sections.

I've been programming professionally since about 1979, and the rules in this book are the ones that I use daily. I make no claims that these rules are definitive or that they're even "correct." I can say, however, that they've served me pretty well over time. Though this book is not a "traps-and-pitfalls" book, many of the rules will keep you out of the sort of trouble that "traps-and-pitfalls" books discuss.

Rules of thumb are, by nature, flexible. They gradually change with experience, and no one rule is valid in every situation; I break my own rules all the time. Nonetheless, I'll warn you at the outset that I'm pretty opinionated about this stuff, and I have little sympathy for sloppy thinking or sloppy programming. I make no apology for stating strongly things that I believe strongly. My opinions are always subject to change, of course, provided that you can convince me that I'm wrong, but bear in mind that this book is based on experience, not theory. I realize that a lot of this book treads dangerously close to religion for some and that many of the things I say are controversial, but I think that there's always room for intelligent discourse between two people with the common goal of improving their craft.

I often teach C++ and object-oriented design classes, both inhouse for individual companies and for the University of California, Berkeley Extension. This book came about at the request of my students, most of whom are dedicated professionals with a real desire to learn the material. I look at a lot of code in the process of grading homework, and this code is pretty representative of the work produced by the professional programming community in the San Francisco Bay area. Unfortunately, every semester, I also see the same problems repeated over and over. This book, then, is in some ways a list of common problems that I find in real code produced by real programmers along with my advice on how to solve those problems.

The programming and design problems discussed here are not limited to student code, unfortunately. Many of the examples of how not to do things are taken from a commercial product: the Microsoft Foundation Class (MFC) library. As far as I can tell, this library was designed without a thought to good maintenance, by people unaware of even rudimentary object-oriented-design principles. I have not explicitly attributed most of these examples in the text because this book is not a "what's wrong with MFC" book; users of the MFC library will recognize the code when they encounter it. I've taken examples from MFC simply because I work with it a lot, so I am very familiar with its foibles. Many other commercial class libraries have similar problems.

Finally, this book is not an introduction to C++. The discussion accompanying the C++-related rules assumes that you know the language. I don't waste space describing how C++ works. There are lots of good books that teach you C++, including my own *C+C++* (New York, McGraw-Hill, 1993). You should also familiarize yourself with object-oriented design principles. I recommend Grady Booch's *Object-Oriented Analysis and Design with Applications*, 2nd ed. (Redwood City, Benjamin Cummings, 1994).

About the rule numbering: Sometimes, I've grouped several rules together because it's convenient to describe them all at the same time. When I've done that, all the rules (which will have different rule numbers) are clumped together at the top of the section. I've used subrules (of the form "1.2") when one rule is a special case of another.

1

The Design Process

This part and the following one on Development are the two most nebulous parts in the book. The rules here are quite general in nature not concerning themselves with the mechanics of C or C++ programming at all, but rather discussing the more general process of program design and development.

The rules in the current part deal with the overall design process. As I reread this part, I become worried that a lot of these rules will seem like platitudes. Nonetheless, some of the rules here are the most important ones in the book, because violating them can cause a lot of grief once development starts. In a way, many of the rules in this part are for managers; programmers often know them but aren't given the freedom to user their knowledge.

1. The essentials of programming: No surprises, minimize coupling, and maximize cohesion.

Many (if not all) of the rules in this book can be summarized into the three meta-rules (if you will) in this section's title.

"No surprises" is self evident. A user interface should act the way it looks like it should act. A function or variable should do what its name implies.

Coupling is a connection between two program or user-interface objects. When an object changes, everything that it's coupled to might change as well. Coupling makes for surprises. (I change this thing over here, and suddenly that thing over there doesn't work.) A C++ example: If an object of one class sends messages to objects of a second class, the sending class is *coupled* to the receiving class. If you change the interface to the receiving class, you'll also have to examine the code in the sending class to make sure it still works. This sort of light coupling is harmless. You do need to know about the coupling relationships to maintain the program, but without some coupling, a program couldn't do anything. Nonetheless, you want to minimize coupling relationships as much as possible.

This minimization is typically done in C using modules and in C++ using classes. The functions in the module (and member functions of the class) are coupled to each other, but with the exception of a few interface functions (or objects), they don't communicate to the outside world at all. In C, you'd use the `static` storage class to restrict the use of a function to a single module. In C++, you use `private` member functions.

Cohesion is the opposite of coupling, things that are grouped together (items in a dialog box, items on a menu, functions in a module, or members of a class) should be related functionally. A lack of cohesion is also "surprising." The editor that I'm using has an "Options" menu, but it also scatters additional configuration options across four other pop-up menus. I expected a cohesive configuration, and when I couldn't find the option I wanted under the "Options" menu, I assumed that the option wasn't available. This bad design is still bothersome; after a year of use I *still* haven't memorized where every option is located, and I often have to spend an annoying five minutes searching in five different places looking for the thing I want to change. On the source-code side, a lack of modular cohesion makes you do the same thing—spending your life looking for function declarations in 15 different files—an obvious maintenance problem.

2. Stamp out the demons of complexity (Part 1).

Richard Rashid (the developer of Mach) gave a keynote address at a Microsoft Developer's Conference a few years ago. His main point was that too much complexity, both in user interfaces and within a program, was the single largest problem facing software designers and users today. Ironically, this speech was given following two days of largely unsuccessful attempts to show several thousand very smart programmers how to program the Microsoft OLE 2.0 interface—one of the most complex application-programming interfaces I've ever seen. (OLE stands for "Object Linking and Embedding." The OLE 2.0 standard defines an interface that two programs can use to interact with each other in an orderly fashion. It's really object orientation at the operating-system level.)

An earlier speaker, who was urging us to use the Microsoft Foundation Class library, told us that MFC's support for OLE "encapsulates 20,000 lines of code *essential* to every basic OLE 2.0 application." The audience was stunned, not by the utility of MFC, but by the fact that it takes 20,000 lines of code to write a basic OLE 2.0 application. Any interface this complex is seriously flawed.

The next few rules use OLE to demonstrate specific problems, but don't think that the complexity problem is Microsoft specific; it's endemic.

2.1 Don't solve problems that don't exist.
2.2 Solve the specific problem, not the general case.

It's instructive to use OLE as an example of what goes wrong with many too-complex designs. There are two main reasons for OLE's complexity. First, it unsuccessfully tries to be language independent. The idea of a C++ virtual-function table is central to OLE 2.0. The OLE specification even uses C++ class notation to document how various OLE interfaces have to work. To implement OLE in a language other than C++, you must simulate a C++ virtual-function table in that language, effectively limiting your choices to C++, C, or assembly language (unless you're a compiler writer and can add features to your language of choice). Frankly, you'd be mad to program OLE in any language other than C++; it will take much less time to learn C++ than it will to write a C++ simulator. This idea of language independence then, is a failure. The interface could be simplified considerably by abandoning it.

Looking back at the story in the previous section, the Microsoft Foundation Classes do actually solve the complexity problem with respect to OLE with a simple, easy-to-understand interface that implements all of the functionality needed by most OLE 2.0 applications. The fact that no one was willing to program OLE until the MFC wrapper layer became available is telling. Providing a good wrapper around a bad interface is no solution to the fundamental problem.

If the MFC wrapper is so simple, then why is the underlying layer so complex? The answer to this question is a basic design issue. The designers of the OLE interface never asked themselves two basic questions:

- What basic functionality does a real application have to support?
- What is the simplest way to implement that functionality?

In other words, they did not have a real application in mind when they designed the interface, but designed for some theoretical worst case. They implemented the most general interface they could without thinking about what was *actually* going to be done with the interface, resulting in a system that could do anything, but that was too complex to be usable. (They probably didn't test the interface by implementing an application in it either, otherwise they would have found these problems.)

In some ways, the object-oriented design process is an attempt to solve this problem. It's relatively easy to add functionality to an object-oriented system, either with derivation or by adding new message handlers to existing classes. By hiding the data definitions from a class's users, you give yourself the ability to completely change the interior organization of a class—including the data definitions—without affecting the users of that class, provided that you maintain the existing interface.

In a structured design, you tend not to have that luxury. You usually design the data structures first, and modifying a data structure is a major undertaking because you have to examine every subroutine that uses that data structure to make sure that it still works. As a consequence, "structured" programs tend to have a lot of code that doesn't do anything. It's there because someone might want to use some functionality in the future. In fact, many structured designers pride themselves on their ability to predict the direction in which the program might evolve. In all, this makes for a lot of needless work and for programs that are bigger than necessary.

Rather than designing for every eventuality, design your code so that it is easily extended when a new functionality is actually needed. Object-oriented designs tend to work better here.

3. A user interface should not look like a computer program (the transparency principle).

I once heard someone say that the best user interface ever designed was the pencil. It's function is immediately clear, it doesn't need a user's manual, it gets the job done with little fuss. The most important attribute, however, is transparency. The pencil, when viewed as an interface between you and the paper, is invisible. When you use a pencil, you are thinking about what you are writing, not about the pencil itself.

Like a pencil, The best computer interfaces are the ones that obscure the fact that you're even talking to a computer: the interface to the ignition system of your car is a great example. You turn on the ignition, put the car in gear, and step on the pedal, as if any of these interface objects (a key, an ignition switch, a pedal) are hooked up directly to the engine. They aren't, though; they're usually just control inputs to a computer which is controlling the engine.

Unfortunately, that level of clarity is often missing from user interfaces. Imagine a Windows GUI interface to an automobile. You start by selecting a main menu called "Move Car." Clicking on it would pop up the "gear shift" menu, which would make you chose from "Forward," "Reverse," and "Neutral." Click one of these to move a check mark next to the desired gear. Then move back up to the main menu and select the "Go" command. This item pops up the "Speed" dialog, where you have to use a slider to enter a desired speed. It's difficult to enter the correct speed, though, because the slider has such fine resolution (1 MPH is about half a millimeter of mouse movement), so you settle for 34.7 MPH rather than 35. You then click the "Go" button on the dialog box, and a message box with an exclamation point pops up saying "The parking break is still engaged—press F1 for help" (and the speaker emits a rude noise). Resigned, you click the "OK" button to get rid of the message box, then try the main menu again, but the machine just beeps at you. Finally realizing that the problem is that the modal "Speed" dialog is still displayed, you click the "CANCEL" button to get rid of it. You pull down the "Parking brake" menu and uncheck the "Engaged" box. You then pull down the "Go" menu again. You get another message box (and rude noise) telling you that you must first select a gear with the "Gear shift" menu. At this point, you decide that maybe you'll walk to work.

Here's another example: In the course of writing a review, I recently looked at several aviation-logbook programs. (A "logbook" is a very simple spreadsheet. Each line represents a particular flight, and the columns break out the total time for the flight into various categories [total time, time spent flying in the clouds, etc.] Other columns mark the flight as business related, and so forth.)

By far, the best interface of the bunch was one that looked just like a familiar paper logbook, but it automated the drudgery. You put a time in the "total" column, and the same time appeared in other likely columns. Columns were added together automatically to form category totals. You could generate the necessary reports easily and export the data to a tab-delimited ASCII format that's readable by virtually every spreadsheet or word-processing program in the world. To an untrained eye, the whole interface seemed underwhelming, to say the least, but it was functional and intuitive, and the program was small and fast. The most important thing, though, is that this interface looked like a logbook, not like a Windows program.

At the other extreme was a wowie-zowie Windows GUI, it had dialog boxes, it had 3-D graphics, you could generate pie charts showing the percentage of cloud time you've had in Cessna 172s in the last 17 years, you could pull up a scanned photograph of an airplane ... you get the picture. The program looked beautiful, but it was almost impossible to use. There was no practical reason to create most of the charts and reports it could generate. Data entry was ungainly and slow; you had to pull down a dialog box with fields scattered all over the place. You actually had to read the whole thing to find the category you were interested in, and some of the categories were hidden under buttons, necessitating an elaborate search. To add insult to injury, the program was built on top of a relational-database server (remember, all this to maintain a simple table with no relational links). It took up 30MB on my disk. It took almost 5 minutes for me to make an entry that takes about 10 seconds to make in the paper logbook or the simple GUI mentioned earlier. The thing was unusable, but it sure was impressive.

One of the main problems was that the tools used to produce the second program drove the interface design. These programs were all developed in a very-high-level language: Visual Basic (which I like quite a bit, by the way). Applications created with application builders such as Visual Basic (or PowerBuilder, or Delphi, or ...) tend to have a particular look that immediately tells you what tool was used to build the application. An interface designer has no recourse if that particular look is inappropriate for a particular design. Users of application generators should have several to chose from, then use the one that best matches the needs of the interface. It's been my experience that most realistic programs will eventually have to move at least some of the interface code into a lower-level language like C or C++, however, so it's important that your application generator be able to use low-level code as well.

4. Don't confuse ease of learning with ease of use.

This problem was once confined almost entirely to the Macintosh, but Windows has been gaining lately. The Mac was designed primarily to be easy to learn. Your great aunt Mathilde MacGilicutty could walk into a computer store and be entering recipes in no time flat. So Mathilde takes the machine home and happily enters recipes for a few months. Now she wants to take her recipes, correlate them based on chemical composition, and write a journal article on the colloidal properties of albumin-based comestibles. Dr. MacGilicutty is a good typist, normally working at about 100 words a minute, but that darn mouse keeps slowing her down. Every time her hands leave the keyboard, she loses a few seconds. She tries to find a word in her document and finds that she has to bring down a menu, enter text in a dialog box, and click several buttons. At the end of the file, she has to explicitly tell the search engine to wrap to the top. (Her 15-year-old version of the vi editor let her do all this with two keystrokes—without letting go of the keyboard.) In the end, she finds that it takes twice as long to perform a common task—writing a journal article—than it used to, mostly because of user-interface problems. She didn't need a manual to use the program, but so what?

Returning to the example of a pencil from the previous section. It's very difficult to learn how to use a pencil. It takes most children several years. (You could argue that many doctors never learn how to use one.) On the other hand, once you learn how, a pencil is very easy to use.

The main issue here is that expert users often require completely different interfaces than beginners. Band aids like hot keys don't solve this problem; the old ungainly user interface is still in the way of productivity, and it makes little difference whether you open a menu with a hot key or the mouse. It's the menu that's the problem.

5. Productivity can be measured in the number of keystrokes.

An interface that requires fewer keystrokes (or other user actions such as mouse clicks) is better than one that requires many keystrokes to perform the same operation, even though these sorts of interfaces tend to be harder to learn.

Similarly, user interfaces that hide information in menus or under buttons are usually harder to use because multiple operations (pulling down several menus) are needed to perform a single task.

Program configuration is a good example. Many of the programs that I use daily scatter configuration options under several menu items. That is, I have to pull down one menu to bring up a dialog box that configures one aspect of what the program does (to choose a font, for example). Then I have to bring down another menu to do something related (to chose a color, for example). It's better to put all configuration options on a single screen and use screen layout to group the options functionally.

6. If you can't say it in English, you can't say it in C/C++.

This rule and the ones that follow are also user-interface rules, but the "user" is the programmer using the code that you're writing—often yourself.

The act of writing out an English description of what a program does, and what each function within the program does, is really a critical step in the thinking process. A well-constructed, grammatically correct sentence is a mark of clear thinking. If you can't write it down, odds are that you haven't fully thought out the problem or the solution. Bad grammar and sentence construction is also an indication of sloppy thinking. The first step of writing any program, then, is to write out what the program does and how it does it.

There is some discussion about whether it's possible to think at all without language, but I'm convinced that analytical thinking of the sort needed in computer programming is closely tied to language skills. I don't think that it's an accident that many of the best programmers that I know have degrees in history, English literature, and the like. It's also not an accident that some of the worst programs I've seen have been written by engineers, physicists, and mathematicians who had devoted a lot of energy in school to staying as far away from English-composition classes as possible.

As a matter of fact, skills in mathematics serve almost no purpose in computer programming. The sort of organizational skills and analytic ability needed for programming come entirely from the Humanities. Logic, for example, was taught by the philosophy department when I was in school. The process used to design and write a computer program is almost identical to the process used to compose and write a book. The process of programming has no connection at all to the process used for solving mathematical equations.

I'm differentiating, here, between computer science—the mathematical analysis of computer programs—and programming or software engineering—a discipline concerned with the writing of computer programs. Programming requires organizational abilities and language skills but not the sort of mathematical abstraction needed to do calculus. (I was forced to take a year of calculus in school but never used any of it in a computer-science class, even though it was a prerequisite to most of them, or in the real world.) Scientists, mathematicians, and engineers who use computers in their work are not necessarily programmers.

I once received a peer review of a book I'd written on the subject of compiler design in which the reviewer (who taught at an Ivy League school) said that he "saw absolutely no relevance in including the source code for a compiler in a book about compiler design." To his mind, one should teach the "basic principles"—the underlying mathematics and language theory—and that the implementation details were "trivial." The first comment makes sense when you realize that it was written by a computer scientist, not a programmer. The reviewer was interested only in the analysis of a compiler, not in how to write one. The second comment just shows you how much the academic elite have isolated themselves from the real work of programming. It's interesting that the original work in language theory that made compiler-writing possible was done by a linguist—Noam Chomsky at M.I.T.—not by a mathematician.

The flip side of this coin is that, when you get stuck solving a problem, one of the best ways to unstick yourself is to explain the problem to a friend. More often than not, the solution springs into your head half way through the explanation.

6.1 Do the comments first.

If you followed the advice in the previous rule, the comments for your program are already done. Just take the implementation description in the document you just wrote and add blocks of code after each paragraph implementing the functionality described in the paragraph. The excuse "I didn't have time to add in the comments" is really saying "I didn't design the code before I wrote it and don't have time to reverse engineer it." If the original programmer can't do this reverse engineering, who can?

7. Read code.

All writers are readers. That's how you learn, by seeing what other writers are doing. Strangely, programmers—who are writers of C++ or C—don't often read code. More's the pity. I strongly suggest that, at minimum, the members of a programming group should read each other's code. The reader can find bugs that you didn't see and make suggestions that will improve the code.

The idea here is not a formal "code critique" which has a judgmental air about it; nobody wants to step on a friend's toes, so the odds of getting useful feedback in a formal situation are small. A better approach is for you to sit down with a friend and just go through the code, explaining what it's doing and getting some feedback and advice. For this exercise to be useful, the code's author shouldn't do any explaining in advance. The reader should be able to understand the code by reading it. (We've all been subjected to textbooks that were so abstruse that we couldn't understand anything until it was explained by a professor. Though this provides job security for the professor, it doesn't reflect well on the book's author.) If you find yourself having to explain something to your reader, that means that your explanation should have been in the code as a comment. Add the comment as you speak; don't put it off until the review is over.

7.1 There's no room for prima donnas in a contemporary programming shop.

This is a corollary to the reading rule. Programmers who think that their code is perfect, who resent criticism rather than taking it as helpful, and who insist that they must work in private, are probably writing unmaintainable gobblygook—even if it does seem to work. (The operative word, here, is *seem*).

8. Decompose complex problems into smaller tasks.

This is really a rule of writing as well. If a concept is too difficult to explain all at once, break it up into smaller parts and explain each part in turn. That's what chapters in a book and sections in a chapter are all about.

To give an example in programming, a threaded binary tree is like a normal tree, except that the child pointers in the leaf nodes point back up into the tree itself. One real advantage of a threaded tree is that it's easy to traverse the tree nonrecursively by following these extra pointers. The problem is that it's difficult to come up with traversal algorithms (postorder traversal in particular). On the other hand, given a pointer to a node, it's easy to write an algorithm that finds its postorder successor. By changing the problem definition from "do a postorder traversal" to "starting at the deepest node, find postorder successors until there are no more," the problem becomes tractable:

```
tree t;
node = postorder_first( t );
while( node )
    node = postorder_successor( t );
```

9. Use the whole language.

9.1 Use the appropriate tool for the job.

This rule is a companion to "Don't confuse familiarity with readability," presented below, but is typically more of a management problem. I've often been told that a student isn't permitted to use some part of C or C++ (typically, it's pointers) because it's "not readable." Usually, this rule is imposed by managers who know FORTRAN, BASIC, or some other language that doesn't support pointers and who can't be bothered to learn C. Rather than admit their knowledge is deficient, these managers would rather hamstring their programmers. Pointers are perfectly readable to a C programmer.

Alternatively, I've seen situations where management required programmers to move from a language like COBOL to C, but weren't willing to pay for the training needed to make the move. Even worse, management paid for the training but weren't willing to budget the time necessary to actually learn the material. Training is a full-time occupation. You can't get "useful" work done simultaneously, and you're throwing away money if you try. Anyway, once the managers see that their staff hasn't been turned into C++ gurus by taking a 3-day short course, they react by limiting the parts of the language that can be used. Effectively saying "You may not use any part of C++ that isn't like the language we used before moving to C++." It certainly won't be possible to exploit any of the advanced features of a language—which are after all the reason for using the language in the first place—if you restrict yourself to the "simplest" feature subset.

Given these limitations, I do wonder why the change from COBOL to C was made in the first place. It's always struck me as lunacy to make COBOL programmers use C. COBOL is a great language for database work. It has built-in primitives that make simple work of tasks that are quite difficult in C. C, after all, was designed to build operating systems, not database application programs. It's easy enough to augment COBOL to support fancy graphical user interfaces if that's the only reason for the move to C.

10. A problem must be thought through before it can be solved.

This rule, and the two that follow, started out at the head of this part of the book. I've moved them here because, on reflection, I was afraid that you'd abandon the whole part after reading them. My intent is not to sermonize, however. These rules address very real problems and, in many ways, are the most important rules in the book.

The current rule is such an obvious statement, when applied to life, that it seems strange that it's almost heresy to apply it to programming. I'm often told that "it's impossible to spend five months in design without writing a line of code—our productivity is measured in lines of code written per day." The people who say this usually know how to do a good design, they just don't have the "luxury."

It's been my experience that a well-designed program not only works better (or works at all) but can be written faster and maintained more easily than a poorly designed one. An extra four months in design can save you more than four months in implementation and could save you literally years of maintenance time. You haven't been very productive if you have to toss out the last year's work because of a fundamental design flaw.

Moreover, poorly designed programs are harder to implement. The argument that you don't have time for design because you "have to get the program market as fast as possible" just doesn't hold water, since it takes much longer to implement a bad (or nonexistent) design.

11. Computer programming is a service industry.

I'm sometimes shocked by the contempt that some programmers have for the users of their programs, as if the "user" (said with a sneer) is a lower life form incapable of cognitive reasoning. The fact is that the entire computer exists for only one purpose: to serve the end users of our products. If nobody used computer programs, there would be no programmers.

The sorry fact is that well over half of the code written every year is discarded. The programs are either never put into service or are used for only a very short time, then discarded. This represents an incredible loss of productivity, dwarfing the day-to-day productivity concerns of most managers. Think of all the startup companies producing programs that will never sell—of all the inhouse development teams writing accounting packages that won't be used.

It's simple to see how this sorry state comes about: programmers are building programs that people don't want. The remedy is also simple, though surprisingly difficult to implement in some environments: ask people what they want, then do what they tell you.

Unfortunately, many programmers seem to believe that end users don't know what they want. Balderdash. More often than not, the users have been so intimidated by the buzzword-rattling "expert" that they clam up. I've often been told "I know what I need, but I can't express it." The best reply to which is, "Well, say it in English; I'll do the translation to Computerish."

12. Involve users in the development process.

13. The customer is always right.

No program can be successful unless the designers talk directly to the end users. Often, however, the situation is more like the game many of us played in kindergarten where 20 kids sat in a circle. Somebody whispers a sentence to his or her neighbor, who relays it to his or her neighbor, and so on around the circle. The fun is in hearing what the message sounds like when it goes full circle— usually nothing like the original message. This same process often happens in program development. A user talks to a manager, who talks to another manager, who hires a consulting company. The president of the consulting company talks to a manager of development, who talks to a team leader, who talks to the programmers. The odds of even a simple requirements document making it through this process unscathed are nil. Even worse, there's almost no way for the developers to ask questions of the end users. The only solution to this problem is to intimately involve users in the development process, ideally by making at least one end user a part of the development team.

A related situation is really just arrogance on the part of the programmer, who says "I know that users say that they want to do it that way, but they don't know enough about computers to make an informed decision; my way is better." This attitude virtually guarantees that the program will never be used. The cure here is to make the end user officially the person who decides that the design is okay. No one can start coding until the user-member of the team signs it off. People who ignore the design in favor of their own concoction should be fired. There's really no room for this sort of child-ish intransigence in the real world.

This is not to say that an experienced designer can't often come up with a better solution to a problem than the one invented by an end user, especially considering that end users often come up with interfaces modeled after programs that they use regularly. You have to convince the user that your way is better before implementing it, however. A "better" interface isn't better if nobody but you can (or will) use it.

14. Small is Beautiful. (Big == slow)

Program bloat is an enormous problem. The 350MB hard disk on my laptop can hold the operating system, a stripped-down version of my compiler, a stripped-down version of my word processor, and nothing else. Back in the dark ages, I could put CP/M versions of all of these on a single 1.2MB floppy. UNIX, at the time, ran quit happily on a 16-bit PDP 11 with 64K of core (internal memory). Nowadays, most operating systems require a 32-bit machine with a minimum of 16MB of core to run at a reasonable speed. I'm convinced that a lot of this memory bloat is the result of sloppy program-ming.

Over and above the space issues, you also have execution-time issues. Virtual memory is not real memory. If your program is too big to fit into core or if it is running simultaneously with other programs, it will have to be swapped to disk periodically. These swaps are time consuming to say the least. The smaller the program, the less likely that a swap will occur, so the faster it tends to run.

The third issue is modularity. One of the basic philosophies of UNIX is that "small is better." Large tasks are best accomplished by a cooperating system of small modular programs, each of which does only one task well, but each of which can communicate with the other components. (Microsoft's Object Linking and Embedding [OLE] standard adds this capability to Windows as does OpenDoc to the Macintosh.) When your application is a modular collection of small programs that work together, it becomes very easy to customize your program by swapping modules. If you don't like the editor, swap in a new one.

Finally, programs tend to get smaller as they are refined. Large programs have probably never gone through the refinement process.

Looking for a solution to this problem, I notice that poorly managed program groups often create unnecessarily large programs. That is, a band of cowboy programmers, each working alone in their office and not talking to one another, will write a lot of redundant code. Instead of one version of a simple workhorse function being used throughout the system, every programmer will create their own version of the same function.

General Development Issues

This part of the book contains rules for the general development process, without getting too much yet into the details of C or C++ themselves. I do that in subsequent parts.

15. First, do no harm.

This rule is for maintenance programming. Back when I was a kid, I read a Science Fiction story where a hapless time traveler accidentally steps on the prehistoric equivalent of a butterfly and returns to his own time to find the world altered in horrible ways. Large computer programs are like that, touch a seemingly insignificant thing over here, and all the code over there stops working. Object-oriented design techniques exist primarily to solve (or at least get a handle on) this problem in the future, but there are millions of lines of legacy code that has to be maintained today.

I've seen programmers change parts of programs just because they don't like the way that the code looks. This is a bad idea. Unless you are familiar with every part of the program that will be effected by a change (and that's almost impossible), don't touch the code. You can quite reasonably argue that virtually none of the rules in this book apply to maintenance programming. You just can't change existing code to bring it into line with any style guide, no matter how much you would like to do so, without running the risk of irrepairable harm. The rules presented here are useful only when you have the luxury of starting from scratch.

16. Edit your code.

17. A program must be written at least twice.

18. You can't measure productivity by volume.

Back when you were taking English in school, you would never have considered handing in the first draft of a writing assignment—at least not if you expected a grade better than a C. Many computer programs are just that, however—first drafts—and they have as many problems as your first-draft essays had. All good code is first written, then edited to make it better. (I mean "edit" in the English sense of "revise," of course.)

Bear in mind that the editing will have to be done eventually because unedited code is essentially unmaintainable (just as your unedited essay was essentially unreadable). The creators of the program are familiar with the code and can do the editing much more efficiently than a maintenance programmer who will first have to decipher the thing before any real work can be done.

Unfortunately, it looks great on a performance review when someone codes quickly but without thought to maintenance or elegance. "Wow, she produces twice the code in half the time." Consider that some poor maintenance programmer will then have to spend eight times as long, reducing the code to half its original size, to get it usable. Lines-of-code per day, a measure of volume, is not a measure of productivity.

If you need motivation other than maintenance, bear in mind that editing can be seen as the process of making something smaller. Small programs run faster.

19. You can't program in isolation.

Gerald Weinberg's classic *The Psychology of Computer Programming* (New York, Van Nostrand Reinhold, 1971) has a great story about soda-pop machines. The powers-that-be in a computing center decided that too much time was being spent hanging out around the pop machines goofing off. People were making too much noise, and getting nothing accomplished, so they removed the machines. Within days, the local consultants became so overloaded with work that people couldn't schedule time with them. The lesson is that people weren't goofing off at all; as they were making all that noise, they were solving each other's problems.

Isolation can be a real problem in an object-oriented design team, which must by necessity be a mix of users, designers, programmers, documenters, and so forth, all working together. Because the number of programmers in the group is often smaller than in a more-traditional design environment, it becomes difficult to find someone with whom to discuss problems; productivity suffers. Think of a weekly company party as a productivity tool.

20. Goof off.

If you can't solve an intractable problem, do something else for a while. Programmers are often most productive when they're staring out of windows, wandering the halls with blank expressions on their faces, sitting in coffee houses drinking Café Lattes, or otherwise "goofing off."

I was a student back in the dark ages when a personal computer was an Apple I, and serious programming geeks owned S-100 boxes that you programmed by entering binary instructions from the front-panel switches, one byte at a time. (If you were lucky, you had a BASIC interpreter and a terminal made out of an old TV set.) The undergraduates shared a PDP 11/70 running UNIX (which ran fine on a 16-bit machine with 64K of memory—My! How things have improved.). Using a PC for your homework was not an option.

The average programming class had between 40 and 80 people in it, and there were six or so programming classes going on at any given moment. Consequently, when an assignment was handed out in class, you grabbed the paper and literally ran as fast as you could down to the terminal room, where you chained yourself to the computer and started coding furiously until you finished the assignment. This could take several days. If you got up to eat or sleep, somebody else got your terminal, and there was a very real possibility that you couldn't get back on in time to get the assignment done. Some people still program this way.

This environment, of course, did not lead to well-thought-out program designs, so most of these programs were four times larger than necessary and took two times longer to debug than was required. Also, the number of lines of code written per hour decreases proportionately with the number hours that you've been sitting staring at a screen. (It's a fantasy to think that you can be more productive working 12 hours a day than working 8.)

At some point during my senior year, I got so frustrated trying to solve a problem that I had been beating my head against for some four hours that I logged off in disgust and stomped out. About three minutes later, while walking down the hill for a knockwurst, the solution popped into my head unbidden. This was a real revelation: you have to relax to let your brain work. Unfortunately, I couldn't get back onto the machine, so I never did fix my bug, but at least I understood how the process should work.

21. Write code with maintenance in mind—the maintenance programmer is you.

Maintenance starts immediately after writing the code, and the maintenance programmer at this stage is usually you. It's a good idea to keep the maintenance programmer happy. Your first concern, then, is for the code to be easy to read. The structure and purpose of every line should be abundantly clear, and when it isn't, you should add explanatory comments.

One of the reasons that the quest for mathematical proofs of program correctness is so quixotic is that there are no correct programs. Not only does every program have bugs, but the requirements change as soon as the program is put into service and the user needs some new feature, thereby introducing new-and-improved bugs. Since the bugs are always with us, we should write our code to make the bugs easier to find.

You could restate the current rule as: Don't be clever. Clever code is hardly ever maintainable.

21.1 Efficiency is often a bugaboo.

I've spent hours making a subroutine more "efficient" without stopping to consider how often that subroutine was called—a waste of time when the routine is called only once or twice. Your code should certainly be as efficient as possible, but your primary concern is maintenance, and you should not sacrifice readability on the altar of efficiency. Code first for maintenance, then run a profiler on your program and find out where the real bottlenecks are. Armed with real information, you now know where's it's worth giving up a little readability in exchange for speed and can go back and make the changes. You might consider putting the original code into a comment, however, so you don't lose it. Always bear in mind that no amount of tweaking at the code level will improve efficiency as much as a better algorithm. A bubble sort is going to run slowly, no matter how well it's coded.

Formatting and Documentation

Formatting is important; C and C++ are hard enough to read as it is without making matters worse with bad formatting. Imagine trying to read a book that had no formatting in it: no paragraph indenting, no blank lines, no capitalization, no spaces following punctuation, and so forth. Maintenance is impossible in poorly formatted code.

I've combined formatting and documentation rules in one part because formatting is one of the best documentation tools at your disposal. The "documentation" discussed in the current part is program documentation (i.e., comments, not user-level documentation.) They don't call it "code" for nothing, and a good comment is your Captain Crunch Secret Decoder Ring.

I realize that debate on formatting and commenting issues approaches religious intensity at times. Bear in mind, then, that the rules I've given here are only the rules that I use. There are other perfectly reasonable ways to do things. On the other hand, some half-wit once told me that "It doesn't matter what formatting style you use, as long as you use it consistently." Code that's formatted consistently bad is worse than code that is occasionally readable. Accidental lucidity is better than none at all.

22. Uncommented code has no value.

A program that takes a year to write could be in use for 10 years. You're going to spend a lot more money on maintenance than you will on the initial creation, and uncommented code is unmaintainable. A "brilliant" programmer who, in one-third the time used by everybody else, writes short, elegant, but uncommented code is costing you money. Some less talented programmer is going to have to spend 10 times longer than necessary fixing the inevitable bugs.

Programmers who can't write English (or whatever language that's spoken in the country where the maintenance is going to go on) are producing time bombs, not computer programs. Since good documentation is so critical to the maintenance process, it's important that programmers be capable of writing it. For this reason, entry-level programmers with degrees in English, history, and other liberal-arts disciplines are often better bets than people with degrees in the hard sciences (math, physics, and so forth.) The hard-science people rarely know how to write, and most of them don't know how to program either; they're taught how to code up an algorithm, not how to write a maintainable computer program.

Fortunately, writing is a skill that is easily learned. Of course, if you follow the "Do the comments first" rule, you'll have all your comments written before you start coding.

23. Put the code and the documentation in the same place.

Once the documentation is separated from the code, it's very difficult to keep it up to date. Consequently, the bulk of your documentation should be in the comments, not in a separate document.

If you really need fancy printed documentation, you can use something like *Web* (for Pascal) or *CWeb* (for C and C++) in conjunction with TeX.[1] I use a similar system called *arachne* that I developed in order to write my book *Compiler Design in C*. (Arachne documents C and C++, using **troff** as the typesetting engine.) All of these programs let you put the source code and documentation in a single file. You can extract the source code to compile it, or you can submit the file to a word processor to print a combined source/documentation manual. The systems allow symbolic cross referencing between the code and document, allow you to reference pieces of code to other pieces of code ("this code is used over there"), and so forth. Because a normal text processor is used for the printed version, you can do things not easy to accomplish in comments—inserting pictures, for example.

24. Comments should be sentences.

They should be properly spelled and punctuated, without abbreviations if possible. Don't turn your comments into a secret code by using strange abbreviations and inventing your own grammatical structure. You shouldn't need that Captain Crunch Secret Decoder Ring to decipher the comments, too.

---

[1]   Web is described in Donald Knuth, *The WEB System of Structured Documentation* (Palo Alto: Stanford University Dept. of Computer Science, Report No. STAN-CS-83-980, 1983). CWeb is described in Donald E. Knuth and Silvio Levy, *The CWEB System of Structured Documentation* (Reading: Addison Wesley, 1994). Both documents not only describe how the system works, but demonstrate it as well. The books document the actual source code using the system that the source code implements.

TeX is Knuth's typesetting system. It is available in several commercial versions.

25. Run your code through a spelling checker.

Not only will your comments be more readable, but this practice will encourage you to use variable names that are readable, because they're actual words. For this reason I suggest not using the check-only-words-in-comments feature available in some editors. Common abbreviations (like `i`, `j`, `p`, `str`, `buf`, etc.) can be added to your spell checker's exception dictionary.

26. A comment shouldn't restate the obvious.

Again, beginning C programmers tend to fall into this trap. Avoid obviously ridiculous thing like:

```
++x;  // increment x
```

but I also don't like comments like:

```
/*-----------------------------------
 * Global-variable Definitions:
 *-----------------------------------
 */
```

Your average programmer knows what a definition looks like.

27. A comment should provide only information needed for maintenance.

A particularly obnoxious, and worthless, comment is the formulaic header block. A header in itself is not evil, quite the contrary. A comment block at the top of a file that describes what's going on in the file can be quite useful. A good one tells you what functionality the file implements, provides a list of public (non `static`) functions, tells you what these functions do, etc.

The headers that I don't like are the ones whose contents are determined by fiat, typically by some sort of company-wide style guide. These sorts of headers usually look like Listing 1, increasing clutter with copious amounts of worthless information at the expense of readability. It is often the case, as in Listing 1, that the header is considerably larger than the actual code. It's also common, as is the case here, that the code is either perfectly self-documenting or needs only a line or two of comments to make it so. Though it might warm the cockles of an autocratic bureaucrat to require this nonsense, it does little to improve maintenance.

Listing 1. A worthless header comment.

```
 1    /*-------------------------------------------------------------**
 2    ** DATE: 29 February, 2000                                     **
 3    **                                                             **
 4    ** FUNCTION:                                                   **
 5    **   equal                                                     **
 6    **                                                             **
 7    ** AUTHOR:                                                     **
 8    **   Joseph Andrews                                            **
 9    **                                                             **
10    ** DESCRIPTION:                                                **
11    **   The purpose of this function is to compare two strings    **
12    **   for lexicographic equality.                               **
13    **                                                             **
14    ** EXCEPTIONS:                                                 **
```

Listing 1. continued...

```
15   **  The function doesn't work for unicode strings.           **
16   **                                                            **
17   **  SPECIAL REQUIREMENTS:                                     **
18   **   none.                                                    **
19   **                                                            **
20   **  ARGUMENTS:                                                **
21   **   char *s1;   A pointer to the first string to compare     **
22   **   char *s2;   A pointer to the second string to compare    **
23   **                                                            **
24   **  OUTPUTS:                                                  **
25   **   The function returns true if the argument strings are    **
26   **   lexicographically identical.                             **
27   **                                                            **
28   **  COMMENTS:                                                 **
29   **   none                                                     **
30   **                                                            **
31   **  IMPLEMENTATION NOTES:                                     **
32   **   None.                                                    **
33   **                                                            **
34   **  REVISION_HISTORY:                                         **
35   **                                                            **
36   **   AUTHOR: Andrews, Joseph                                  **
37   **   DATE:   12, July, 1743                                   **
38   **   CHANGE: Initial                                          **
39   **                                                            **
40   **   AUTHOR: Jones, Tom                                       **
41   **   DATE:   13, July,  1743                                  **
42   **   CHANGE: Changed names of arguments from str1, str2.      **
43   **                                                            **
44   ** All code in this file is copyright (c) Fictitious Inc.     **
45   **              All rights reserved.                          **
46   **                                                            **
47   ** No part of this subroutine may be reproduced in any form **
48   ** whatsoever without explicit permission in triplicate from**
49   ** the department of redundancy department. Violators will   **
50   ** be required to hand over their firstborn male child.      **
51   **----------------------------------------------------------**
52   */
53   inline equal( char *s1, char *s2 )
54   {
55       return !strcmp(s1,s2); // Return true if strings are equal.
56   }
```

The real problem is that this sort of header violates many other rules: "don't comment the obvious," "eliminate clutter," and so forth. What little real information that is supplied in the header belongs in a revision-control system, not in the source code. Comments in the code should tell you things that are useful for maintenance.

28. Comments should be in blocks.

Comments are generally best if placed in multiline blocks alternating with blocks of code. That is, the comment should be describing at a high level what the next several lines are doing. If every other line is a comment, it's like reading two books at the same time, one line from the first, then one line from the second, and so on. If the code that you're commenting is complex, you can use footnotes:

```
// Here is a block comment describing the block of code that follows.
// After a general summary, I describe some specifics:
//
//    1. This comment describes what's happening on the line
//       labeled with a 1
//
//    2. This comment describes what's happening on the line
//       labeled with a 2
//
// At point 1, below, the algorithm is positioned to...
//

here_is_the_code();
while( some_condition )
{
    this_code_is_rather_obscure();        /* 1 */
}
more_stuff_here();
while( some_condition )
{
    this_code_is_also_obscure();          /* 2 */
}
```

29. Comments should align vertically.

Align the /* and */ vertically in multiline comments.

```
/* First line,
 * second line,
 * third line.
 */
```

If your compiler supports it, C++ style comments help here:

```
// First line,
// second line,
// third line.
```

There are two reasons for this rule, both demonstrated in the following code:

```
/********************************************************************

void the_function( void )

    Here is a multiline comment, doing all of the things that a comment
    should do.

    Unfortunately, the lack of a vertical line of stars to the left
    makes it difficult to visually separate the comment from
    the code

 *********************************************************************

void the_function( void )
{
    // here is the actual function.

    code_goes_here();
}

/********************************************************************/
```

First, did you notice that I forgot to put a / at the far right of the second line of stars? It's easy to lose entire functions this way. Second, it's hard to see where the comment stops and the code begins. Fix both problems as follows:

```
/********************************************************************
 * void the_function( void )
 *
 *   Here is a multiline comment, doing all of the things that a comment
 *   should do.
 *
 *   The vertical line of stars to the left makes it
 *   easy to visually separate the comment from the code
 *
 ********************************************************************
 */

void the_function( void )
{
    // here is the actual function.

    code_goes_here();
}
```

30. Use neat columns as much as possible.

Because formatting is really a kind of comment, the foregoing rule applies to the actual code as well. The following two blocks are functionally identical, but note how much easier it is to find variable names in the second block, not just because of the comment alignment, but because the names fall into a neat column as well:

```
int x; // Describe what x does.
unsigned long int (*pfi)(); // Describe what pfi does.
const char *the_variable; // Describe what the_variable does.
int z; // Describe what z does.
x = 10; // Comment goes here
the_variable = x; // Another comment goes here
z = x; // Here's another.
```

as compared to:

```
int             x;              // Describe what x does.
unsigned long int ( *pfi )();   // Describe what pfi does.
int             z;              // Describe what z does.

const char      *the_variable;  // Describe what the_variable does.

x            = 10;              // Comment goes here
the_variable = x;               // Another comment goes here
z            = x;               // Here's another.
```

You can look at this sort of formatting as "tabular" in nature, as if I was creating a table with a "type" column, a "name" column, and a "description" column.

Another good use of columns is in a C++ member-initialization list, which I format as follows:

```
class derived : public base
{
    string      str;
    const int   x;
public:
    derived( char *init_str, int init_x ){}
}

derived::derived( char *init_str, int init_x )
                            :base( str, x   )
                            ,str ( init_str )
                            ,x   ( init_x   )
{}
```

31. Don't put comments between the function name and the open brace.

The main problem with:

```
foo( int x )
/*  Don't put
 *  comments
 */ here.
{
    //...
}
```

is that the function body might end up on the next screen or page. Also, readers can't easily tell whether they're looking at a prototype or an actual definition. Move the comment either above the function name or into the function body beneath the open brace:

```
/* Either put
** it here.
*/

foo( int x )
{
    /* Or put it here,
    ** indented at the same level as the code.
    */
}
```

32. Mark the ends of *long* compound statements with something reasonable.

First of all, end-of-block comments such as:

```
while( a < b )
{
    for( i = 10; --i >= 0; )
    {
        f( i );
    } // for
} // while
```

do nothing but add clutter when the blocks are short. I use them only when the compound statement is too large to fit on a screen (in my editor about 40 lines) or when there is so much nesting that I can't keep track of what's going on. End-of-block comments are certainly worthwhile when the compound statements are large, but I've often seen code like this:

On page 1:

```
while( a < b )
{
    while( something_else() )
    {
        for( i = 10; --i >= 0; )
        {
            for( j = 10; --j >= 0; )
            {
                // lots of code goes here
```

On some subsequent page:

```
            } // for
        } // for
    } // while
} // while
```

These comments are too terse to be useful. End-of-block comments should identify the controlling statement completely. The end-of-block comments from the previous example should look like this:

```
            } //      for( j = 10; --j >= 0; )
        }     //      for( i = 10; --i >= 0; )
    }         //      while( something_else() )
}             // while( a < b )
```

Because an `#ifdef` is almost always some distance from the `#endif`, I always label the `#endif`:

```
#ifndef __SOMEFILE_H_
#define __SOMEFILE_H_

// 1000 lines of code go here

#endif // __SOMEFILE_H_
```

I'll do the same with a `#else`.

33. Put only one statement per line.

There's absolutely no reason to pack as much stuff on one line as you can, unless you intend to make the code unreadable. If there's more than one semicolon on a line, something's wrong. Don't use a comma operator (even if you know what it is) for the same reason. An obvious exception is the `for` statement, all three parts of which should be on a single line.

34. Put argument names in function prototypes.

This is particularly important in class definitions. Manual pages (and help systems) for the code you're working on hardly ever exist when you most need them—as you're doing the initial development. You typically get the documentation from two places: comments attached to the actual functions and *.h* files. Of the two, the *.h* file is usually better because it's more compact. In any event, the documentation you usually need for a function is the order and number of arguments, and the easiest place to find this information is in the function prototype. If your prototypes look like this:

```
some_function( int, int, int, int, int );
```

you're not going to get much help.

35. Use a "predicate" form to split up long expressions.

A "predicate" in English is the back half of the sentence—the verb and the object on which the verb is acting. Word order in English is, of course, inflexible: the verb always comes first.

Many computer languages actually mimic the structure of English (C and C++ fall into this category). Pascal, for example, is even punctuated like an English sentence, with semicolons separating independent clauses and a period at the end of the whole shebang. A function call is a good example of a predicate form: the verb is the function name and the direct objects (the things on which the verb is acting) are the arguments.

You can also look at operators as verbs, because they perform some action on the operands (the "objects"). It's reasonable, then, to use the same layout that you would with an English sentence when you need to split a long expression onto several lines. Put the verb (the operator) first:

```
if(    its_thursday_and_the_moon_is_in_scorpio()
    || its_friday_afternoon_and_close_to_quitting_time()
    || i_just_cant_bear_to_look_at_this_computer_for_another_minute()
  )
{
    go_home();
}
```

Of course, you might be better off just shortening the subroutine names to something more reasonable so that they'll all fit on one line.

Notice how I've placed the parentheses and braces in the earlier code to make the structure more apparent. Also notice that I've used braces, even though the language doesn't require it, to make it easier to find the statement attached to the `if`. The following code is harder to read because it's more difficult to see where the `if` ends and the statement begins:

```
if(    its_thursday_and_the_moon_is_in_scorpio()
    || its_friday_afternoon_and_close_to_quitting_time()
    || i_just_cant_bear_to_look_at_this_computer_for_another_minute() )
    go_home();
```

36. A subroutine should fit on a screen.

The subroutine-calling overhead in C/C++ is quite small; if the function is `inline`, it's nil. It's a good idea, then, to make your subroutines a manageable size and also to use a lot of them. A subroutine name makes a great abstraction. If the names are chosen properly, you can often eliminate the need for comments.

In general, I like for the working part of a subroutine (the code, less the header comments and so forth) to be visible in its entirety when I'm editing; it should fit on one screen or one window.

37. All code should be printable.

It's often easier to debug from a printed page than from a screen, even a large screen. The paper is easier to read because it's higher resolution and in sharper focus than the screen. You also can spread out the paper listings on a table top. You can't get that kind of concurrency unless you have having 3-by-5-foot, 300-dpi monitor.

So, your code should be easily printable. Subroutines should fit on a single page if possible (about 60 lines max), and no line of code should be so long that it can't fit on a single line of output (about 79 characters, depending on the font), even if your editor does scroll horizontally. If you exceed these limits, you have to use such a small font to get everything to fit that you can't read the listings any more.

38. Use lines of dashes for visual separation between subroutines.

I always put a comment like:

```
//-------------------------------------------------------------
```

above every function definition. (By extension, I don't use lines of dashes anywhere else.) Though blank lines are great for providing visual separation between block of code, if you use blank lines exclusively, they stop working. A line of dashes between functions makes it very easy to find the functions. Just as a blank line represents a paragraph boundary, dashed lines are like section headings. When I need even further separation, I use:

```
//=============================================================
// DESCRIPTIVE TEXT
//=============================================================
```

Think of it as a chapter heading.

I try not to put any comments except dashed lines at this outermost nesting level because such comments can make it difficult to find the function definitions. That is, I format functions like this:

```
//------------------------------------------------------------
void descriptive_name( type descriptive_name )
{
    // If the function and argument names are not sufficiently
    // descriptive, I'll put a comment here describing what the
    // function does. I'll omit this comment if the names are
    // adequate to get the point across. (The relevant rule is
    // "Don't comment the obvious.")
    //
    // I describe the return values and argument next. Again
    // you might not need this comment if the names are good
    // enough.
    //
    // Finally, I put a comment here describing how the function
    // does whatever it does. Again, I'll leave this comment out
    // when the code itself is sufficiently descriptive.

    code_goes_here();
}
```

39. White space is one of the most effective comments.

This seems like a small issue, but it can dramatically improve the readability of your code. Look at how white space is used in this book as an organizational device and you'll see how to use it in your own programs. Blank lines (or an indented first line) give visual separation between paragraphs. A space follows a period, but doesn't precede it, because the period terminates something. You get the idea. Here are the rules:

- Break the code into logical chunks (i.e. paragraphs) where each chunk performs one operation. Surround those chunks with either blank lines or lines containing only a curly brace.
- White space should always follow punctuation.
- Operators are abbreviations for words. When you see "+," you say "plus." Like any abbreviation, you should surround the symbol with space characters. (For example: a + b reads "a plus b," a+b reads "aplusb.")
- Exceptions are unary operators, which are treated as word prefixes or suffixes (*p, a--, f(arg, arg), etc).
- A . or -> is the C/C++ equivalent of a hyphen. There should be no space on either side: p->msg(),obj.msg().

Here's one of the things that happens when you pack things too tightly. Consider:

```
int *p;
y=(x/*p++);
f(int /* place-holder */);
```

When you strip the comments out, you get:

```
int *p;
y=(x
              );
```

The `/*` in `y=(x/*p++)` is treated as a start-of-comment symbol that is terminated by the `*/` in the `f()` call. (This one really happened to me, and it took all day to track it down. The compiler, of course, generated no error messages because there's nothing syntactically incorrect.)

One final related issue. I've been seeing declarations like the following a lot lately:

```
int*    x;
```

The problem is that:

```
int*    x, y;
```

does not declare two pointers, as the distribution of white space implies. This is really another I-can-program-FORTRAN-in-any-language problem. Though it would be nice if C worked in the way the foregoing formatting implies, it doesn't. When properly formatted,

```
int     *x, y;
```

makes it very clear that x is a pointer and y isn't

40. Use four-space indents.

Nickolaus Wirth, who invented Pascal and Modula-2, once published a book that used one-space indents throughout the book. The listings were some of the hardest reading I've ever done. Use enough indent so that your reader can tell the code is indented; four spaces seem ideal.

You must indent consistently. Even the outer block of a subroutine should be indented. This is not acceptable:

```
void f(void)
{
if( x )
    yyy();
more_code();
even_more_code();
}
```

because it makes it too hard to find the top of the subroutine. Compare the foregoing to the following:

```
void f(void)
{
    if( x )
        yyy();
    more_code();
    even_more_code();
}
```

41. Indent statements associated with a flow-control statement.

I do this even with one-line statements:

```
if( by_land )
    one();
else
    two();
```

not:

```
if( by_land ) one() else two();
```

One obvious exception is:

```
if( by_land )
{
    one();
}
else if( by_sea )
{
    two();
}
else if( by_air )
{
    three();
}
```

I've used braces here for two reasons. First, I've occasionally thrown in an `if` statement while debugging and forgotten to put in the brace, as in the following code:

```
if( by_land )
    one();                          if(debug) printf("aagh");
else if( by_see )
```

which binds like this:

```
if( by_land )
    one();

if(debug)
    printf("aagh");
else
    if( by_see )
```

Code is also more readable if the braces are there.

I sometimes violate the indenting rule when I can use formatting to make it crystal clear what's going on. The neat columns make the following workable:

```
if        ( by_land  ) one();
else if ( by_sea    ) two();
else if ( by_tunnel ) three();
```

but this is unreadable:

```
if(by_land)one();
else if(by_sea)two();
else if(by_tunnel)three();
```

Code like the following isn't acceptable:

```
for( a ; b ; c );
while( ++i < 10 );
```

It's too easy to accidentally do:

```
while( i < 10 );
    ++i;
```

(In other words "compare i to 10 forever, then increment i.") If a semicolon never appears at the end of a line that starts with a for or while, you can use a search-file-for-string utility like **grep** to find these problems for you.

41.1 Comments should be at the same indent level as the surrounding code.

The whole point of indenting is to make your code's structure readily apparent. If you indent comments in a helter-skelter fashion, you've defeated the purpose of the indenting. The comment in the following code should be indented:

```
f()
{
/* A longish comment
** goes here.
*/
    code();
}
```

A similar problem is:

```
f()
{
int local_var;
int another_local_var;
    code();
}
```

Not indenting the local-variable definitions implies that they are at the same scoping level as the function name (which is global). Because this isn't true, you should indent to indicate scope:

```
f()
{
    int local_var;
    int another_local_var;

    code();
}
```

42. Align braces vertically at the outer level.

Finding a missing curly brace is sometimes a big problem. If you hang the braces out where you can see them, it's easier to see when they're mismatched:

```
while( some_condition )
{
    // inner block
}
```

I really dislike the "K&R" style of:

```
if( condition {
    code();
}else{
    more_code();
}
```

Not only is it hard to match up the braces, but the lack of visual separation provided by a line containing only an open brace makes for less readability.

43. Use braces when more than one line is present under a flow-control statement.

This rule applies even when the additional lines are only comments. The problem is that it's too easy to accidentally add another statement and forget to add the braces. Code like the following is safer:

```
if( something() )
{
    /* Quo usque tandem abutere
     * Gatesalina, patientia
     * nostra
     */
    something_else();
}
```

Names and Identifiers

Names are important. Properly chosen names can make the code virtually self documenting, requiring little or no extra input in the guise of explicit comments. Poorly chosen names (like `state`) can add unnecessary complexity to your code. This part of the book contains rules that are specific to naming.

44. Names should be common English words, descriptive of what the function, argument, or variable does.

Avoid abbreviations; they hurt readability. Some people abbreviate habitually, leading to absurd practices like truncating the last letter from a word or removing all vowels from a word. Consider the oddly named UNIX `creat()` function; `create()` is obviously better. I've also seen ridiculous things like `lngth` for `length` and `mt` for `empty`.

Abbreviations in common use are obvious exceptions. Here are a few that I see enough that I use them myself:

`col`	column index
`cur`	current
`i j`	generic loop counter
`max`	maximum (usually as a prefix or suffix)
`min`	minimum (usually as a prefix or suffix)
`obj`	generic object (you have base-class pointer but don't know derived class).
`p ptr`	generic pointer
`s str`	string (typically a `char*` in C)

but don't use these if the named object is not being used in a generic way. For example, `i` makes sense for a loop counter in a `for` statement only if that counter is used for no other purpose than counting the number of iterations:

```
for( i = 10; --i >= 0; )     // draw 10 dashes
    putchar('-');
```

Use a real name when you use the counter for something other than counting. Compare this code:

```
for( i = 0; i < imax; ++i )
    for( j = 0; j < jmax; ++j )
        move_cursor(i,j);
```

to:

```
for( row = 0; row < max_row; ++row )
    for( col = 0; col < max_col; ++col )
        move_cursor( row, col );
```

I'd also avoid `x` and `y` when you mean `row` and `column`. An earlier rule recommended running your code through a spelling checker. A real benefit of this practice is that it encourages you to use real words for names.

44.1 Do not clutter names with gibberish.

A great example of this problem can be seen in any Microsoft-supplied sample code, though the problem is by no means restricted to Microsoft. All Microsoft Windows demonstration code encodes a variable's type into its name. For example, a declaration like the following:

```
const char *str;
```

would be declared like this:

```
LPCSTR lpszstr;
```

Translate `lpszstr` as: "long pointer to string terminated by zero called `str`." There are actually several problems, here, not the least of which is the fact that the LPCSTR hides the fact that we're declaring a pointer. The problem addressed by the current rule is the name itself, however.

This naming style is called "Hungarian" notation, after the native country of Microsoft's head of programming, Charles Simonyi, who invented it. (It's not called Hungarian notation because it makes Microsoft code look as if it were written in Hungarian.)

Hungarian notation makes a lot of sense in assembly language, in which all you know about a variable is its size. Encoding type information in the name tells you how the variable is used as well.[2] Higher-level languages like C and C++ use variable declarations for this purpose.

Dr. Simonyi has defended the notation in print several times, but I see little to recommend it in a C or C++ program. To my mind, Hungarian notation does nothing but hurt readability. A simple str or string is much more readable and conveys the same information. If you really need to know the type, it's easy enough to find the definition.[3]

It is also a common, though less extreme, practice to start pointer names with p. This practice also just clutters the code. You probably don't start ints with i, doubles with d, and functions with f. Why use p for pointers? The one obvious exception is when you have both an object and a pointer to the object in the same scope:

```
char    str[128], *pstr = str;
```

On the other hand, a real name for the pointer is probably better. Consider:

```
char    str[128], *first_nonwhite = str;
while( isspace(*first_nonwhite) )
    ++first_nonwhite;

// At this juncture, the name "first_nonwhite" tells you a lot
// more about what the variable's doing than would "pstr."
```

45. Macro names should be ENTIRELY_CAPITALIZED.

As is discussed in a subsequent section, macros often have side effects. It's useful, then, to be able to tell at a glance that something is a macro. Of course, you shouldn't use all caps for anything except macros or you've defeated the purpose of the current rule.

45.1 Do not capitalize members of an enum.

It should be possible to replace a constant defined with an enum with a const variable. If the name is all caps, you'd then have to change the name. There are also macro-related problems (which will be discussed shortly) that don't exist with an enum. It's useful to distinguishing the two with a glance.

---

2   I suspect that Hungarian notation came to be used so heavily because much of Microsoft Windows is written in assembly language.

3   At least it should be. I suspect that some proponents of Hungarian notation organize their code so poorly that they can't find the declarations. By encoding the type in the name, they can save hours of searching around in poorly constructed listings. Assembly language programs, which tend by necessity to have large numbers of global variables, are an obvious exception.

45.2 Do not capitalize type names created with a `typedef`.

Because a macro can also be used in a `typedef`-like manner, it's useful to know whether or not something can be used syntactically as a true type. For example, given:

```
typedef void (*ptr_to_funct)(int);
```

you can say both of the following:

```
(ptr_to_funct)( p );     // cast p into a function pointer
ptr_to_funct f(long);    // f returns a function pointer
```

A macro like:

```
#define PTR_TO_FUNCTION void(*)(int)
```

lets you do the cast:

```
(PTR_TO_FUNCTION)( p );
```

but not the function declaration:

```
PTR_TO_FUNCTION f(long);
```

The macro expands to:

```
void(*)(int) f(long);
```

but the compiler wants:

```
void (*f(long))(int);
```

A lower case type name doesn't pose any reading problems because you can always tell by context whether or not a symbol is used as a type.

46. Avoid the ANSI C name space.

Symbols starting with underscores and type names ending with _t have been reserved in ANSI C for use by the compiler vendor. Don't do either. Also, avoid any function name that is part of the ANSI C or Draft ISO/ANSI C++ standard.

47. Avoid the Microsoft name space.

This might seem like a Microsoft-specific rule, but it isn't (given Microsoft's current proclivities towards world dominion). Anyone who's serious about portability must consider that his or her code might eventually either run under a Microsoft operating system or have to interface to a Microsoft class library. The Foundation Class Library, for example, has been ported to the Macintosh and many UNIX/Motif environments at this writing and will probably appear on other operating systems in the near future.

At this writing the Windows application-programming interface (API) has some 1,200 functions in it. The Microsoft Foundation Class (MFC) library, which is rapidly supplanting the raw C interface, adds some 80 class definitions. Unfortunately, Microsoft has a way of adding even more functions and classes with almost every release of the compiler. If Microsoft happens to pick a function or class name that you're using for some other purpose, guess who's going to have to change the name.

Because none of these Microsoft symbols conform to the ANSI C standard, which requires the names of vendor-supplied objects to begin with an underscore, you must protect yourself by avoiding Microsoft-style naming conventions:

- All Microsoft function names use Pascal-style conventions of `MixedUpperAndLowerCase()`, and they always start with a capital letter. I prefer all lowercase and underscores, but whatever you do, `DontUseTheMicrosoftStyle()`. Member functions in MFC classes follow the same convention.
- Microsoft class names all start with a capital "C" followed by another capital letter (for example, `CString, CWnd, CDialog`, etc.). The initial C does little but add clutter, and omitting it from our own names gets us out of the Microsoft name space.
- One of the most basic precepts of object-oriented design is not to expose member data in class definitions. Nonetheless, many Microsoft Foundation Class classes have `public` data fields. These fields all start with an `m_`, which serves no purpose other than adding clutter to the name. Nonetheless, we can exploit this nonsense by not starting our own field names with `m_`, thus easily distinguishing our members from those inherited from the MFC base class.

48. Avoid unnecessary symbols.

Symbolic constants are often introduced unnecessarily. For example, don't define error return values if only one error is returned, just return FALSE. Don't do this:

```
enum { INSERT_ERROR, DELETE_ERROR };

insert()
{
    //...
    return INSERT_ERROR;
}

delete()
{
    //...
    return DELETE_ERROR;
}
```

just return 0 on failure and some true value like 1 on success.

49. Symbolic constants for Boolean values are rarely necessary.

Choosing a wrong name can add a lot of unnecessary complexity to your code. Consider the following simplistic function that counts words in a string:

```
int nwords(const char *str)
{
    typedef enum { IN_WORD, BETWEEN_WORDS } wstate;

    int     word_count  = 0;
    wstate  state       = BETWEEN_WORDS;

    for(; *str ; ++str )
    {
        if( isspace(*str) )
            state = BETWEEN_WORDS;
        else
            if( state != IN_WORD )
            {
                ++word_count;
                state = IN_WORD;
            }
    }
    return word_count;
}
```

The improperly chosen name, state has required us to introduce two unnecessary symbols:
IN_WORD and BETWEEN_WORDS. Now consider this variant:

```
int nwords2(const char *str)
{
    int word_count  = 0;
    int in_word     = 0;

    for(; *str ; ++str )
    {
        if( isspace(*str) )
            in_word = 0;
        else
            if( !in_word )
            {
                ++word_count;
                in_word = 1;
            }
    }
    return word_count;
}
```

Renaming the nebulously named state to something that actually describes what the variable is
doing lets me eliminate the Boolean symbolic constants IN_WORD and BETWEEN_WORDS. The resulting subroutine is both smaller and easier to read.

Here's another example. The following code:

```
enum child_type { I_AM_A_LEFT_CHILD, I_AM_A_RIGHT_CHILD };
struct tnode
{
    child_type   position;
    struct tnode *left,
                 *right;
} t;
//...

t.position = I_AM_LEFT_CHILD;

if( t.position == I_AM_LEFT_CHILD )
    //...
```

can be simplified like this:

```
struct tnode
{
    unsigned     is_left_child ;
    struct tnode *left,
                 *right;
} t;

t.is_left_child = 1;

if( t.is_left_child )
    //...
```

thereby eliminating two unnecessary symbols. One final example is:

```
enum { SOME_BEHAVIOR, SOME_OTHER_BEHAVIOR, SOME_THIRD_BEHAVIOR };

f( SOME_BEHAVIOR      , x);
f( SOME_OTHER_BEHAVIOR, x);
f( SOME_THIRD_BEHAVIOR, x);
```

which requires four symbols (three symbolic constants and a function name). It's better, though sometimes impossible, to eliminate the selector constant in favor of multiple functions:

```
some_behavior(x);
some_other_behavior(x);
some_third_behavior(x);
```

The flip side of this coin is in a function call. Consider this prototype:

```
create_window( int has_border, int is_scrollable, int is_maximized );
```

I've again chosen reasonable names to eliminate the need for symbolic constants. Unfortunately, the function call is unreadable:

```
create_window( TRUE, FALSE, TRUE );
```

I have no idea what the window will look like from just looking at the call. A few symbolic constants clean things up in the call:

```
enum { UNBORDERED  =0, BORDERED   =1};   // Must have values shown
enum { UNSCROLLABLE=0, SCROLLABLE =1};   // or create_window()
enum { NORMAL_SIZE =0, MAXIMIZED  =1};   // won't work.
//..
create_window( BORDERED, UNSCROLLABLE, MAXIMIZED );
```

but now I've a different problem. I don't want to use the symbolic constants inside create_window() itself. They're here only to make the call more readable, and I don't want to clutter up the function with code like:

```
if( has_border == BORDERED )
    //...
```

as compared to a simple:

```
if( has_border )
    //...
```

The former is both ugly and redundant. Unfortunately, if someone changes the value of the symbolic constant BORDERED, the second if statement won't work. I usually compromise with a comment that tells the maintenance programmer not to change the symbol values, as I've done in the previous example.

Rules for General Programming

This part contains rules that affect coding generally, as compared to the earlier part that discussed program development generally. These rules aren't particularly language dependent.

50. Don't confuse familiarity with readability.

(Or the real-programmers-can-program-FORTRAN-in-any-language syndrome.) Many people attempt to abuse the macro preprocessor to make C look like some other language. For example:

```
#define begin {
#define end   }

while( ... )
begin
    //...
end
```

This practice does nothing but make your code unreadable to someone who doesn't know the language you're trying to mimic. It makes the code less readable to a C programmer, not more so.

A related problem is using the macro preprocessor to hide the C declaration syntax. For example, don't do the following:

```
typedef const char *LPCSTR;

LPCSTR str;
```

This sort of thing causes maintenance problems because someone not familiar with your conventions will have to look up the `typedef` to find out what's really going on. Additional confusion arises in C++, because the reader might interpret the foregoing as a definition for a C++ object of class LPCSTR. It will not occur to most C++ programmers that an LPCSTR is a pointer. C declarations are perfectly easy to read by C programmers. (Don't, by the way, confuse the foregoing with the reasonable practice of defining word as a 16-bit signed number to get around the portability problems inherent in an `int`, whose size is undefined in ANSI C and in C++).

By the same token, many programmers avoid the conditional operator (`?:`) just because they think it looks weird. The conditional can simplify your code considerably, however, and make the code more readable as a consequence. There are a lot of examples of the conditional scattered throughout this book, but here's one to make my point: I think that:

```
printf("%s", str ? str : "<empty>");
```

is much more elegant than:

```
if( str == NULL )
    printf( "<empty>" );
else
    printf( "%s", str );
```

You also save the overhead of two `printf()` calls.

I also often see `++` and `--` used incorrectly. The whole point of an autoincrement or autodecrement is to combine the operation with other operations. Instead of:

```
while( *p )
{
    putchar( *p );
    ++p;
}
```

or:

```
for( ; *p ; ++p )
    putchar( *p );
```

use:

```
while( *p )
    putchar( *p++ );
```

This code is perfectly readable to a competent C programmer, even if there's no equivalent operation in FORTRAN or Pascal.

You should also never hide operators in macros just because you don't like the way they look. I once saw the following in a real program:

```
struct tree_node
{
    struct tree_node *lftchld;
};

#define left_child(x)    ((x)->lftchld)
//...
traverse( tree_node *root )
{
    if( left_child(root) )
        traverse( left_child( root ) );
    //...
}
```

The programmer deliberately made the structure definition less readable to avoid a name conflict between a field and a completely unnecessary macro, all because he didn't like the look of the -> operator. He would have been much better off just calling the field left_child and dispensing with the macro altogether.

If you really think that a program must look like Pascal to be readable, you should be programming in Pascal, not C or C++.

51. A function should do only one thing.

It's usually a bad idea to encode what a function is supposed to do in its arguments. The function name should do this. For example:

```
UpdateAllViews( CView *sender, long lhint, CObject *phint )
{
    // sender   lhint   phint
    // NULL     xx      xx      Initial update, called from framework
    // CView*   0       CRect*  Called when embedded object invalidated.
    //                          phint points at document-relative rectangle
    //                          holding position of invalid object.
    // CView*   1       CRect*  Message sent by CView object ("sender")
    //                          phint holds client frame of the CView.
    //...
}
```

You should have three functions here: initial_update(), update_embedded_object(), and update_view(). One sure clue that something's wrong here is the nebulous nature of the argument names. A function shouldn't be passed "hints." It should be given directives.

52. Too many levels of abstraction or encapsulation are as bad as too few.

The main point of using abstractions, such as functions or symbolic constants (or encapsulations like `struct` or `class` definitions) is to make the code more readable. Don't use them just because you can. For example, the nested `struct`s in the following code serve no useful purpose:

```
struct tree_node;

struct child_ptr
{
    unsigned        is_thread;
    struct tree_node *child;
};

struct tree_node
{
    struct child_ptr left,
                     right;
};

tree_node *p;
if( !p->left.am_a_thread )
    p = p->left.child;
```

The following is more readable because there are fewer dots and is easier to maintain because there's one fewer definition to debug:

```
struct tree_node
{
    struct tree_node *left_child;
    unsigned         left_is_thread  : 1;

    struct tree_node *right_child;
    unsigned         right_is_thread : 1;
};

if( !p->left_is_thread )
    p = p->left_child;
```

53. A function should be called more than once, but...

By the same token, if a function is properly cohesive (i.e. if it performs a single operation and all of the code in the function works towards that end), there's no reason to break out a chunk of code into other functions unless you will use the broken-out code somewhere else. My experience is that, when a function gets too large, it's often possible to break out pieces that are general enough to be reused elsewhere in the program, so this rule doesn't really contradict the "small is beautiful" rule. If you don't break out the code, a block comment describing the purpose of the block of code that you would have broken out serves the same purpose as the function name—documentation.

There are times, however, when breaking out code into a smaller function makes the code dramatically more readable because of the eliminated clutter. This practice—abstracting a chunk of code into a single function name—does add symbols to the global name space, however, and the added overall complexity is a definite minus. When I do use a function in this way—as an abstraction—I generally declare it both `static`, so it can't be accessed outside the current file, and `inline`, so there won't be any overhead in the call. Don't take the function-as-abstraction process to an extreme. I've seen perfectly good programs rendered completely unreadable by abstracting things to the point where no function was longer than five or six lines. The resulting program also ran much slower than necessary, and the source code was five times longer than it needed to be.

53.1 Code used more than once should be put into a function.

This rule is the flip side of the previous one. If you find almost-identical code appearing in more than one place in your program, this code should be split out into a subroutine that's called from several places. The benefits are smaller program size and better maintenance, the latter both because the program is simpler and because you now have only one function to maintain; if you find a bug, you need to fix it in only one place. As mentioned earlier, the function name provides a good abstraction as well. Calls to a well named function are usually self explanatory, obviating the need for a comment.

54. A function should have only one exit point.

This rule applies only to C programs. Generally, multiple `goto` branches to a single exit point are better than multiple return statements. This way you can put a breakpoint at the single exit point rather than having to deal with multiple breakpoints. For example:

```
f()
{
    int ret_val = ERROR;

    if( some_condition )
    {
        //...
        ret_val = SOMETHING;
        goto exit;
    }
    else
    {
        //...
        ret_val = SOMETHING_ELSE;
        goto exit;
    }

exit:
    return ret_val;
}
```

This technique doesn't work in C++ because constructor functions are called implicitly as part of a declaration; a declaration often hides a function call. If you skip over the declaration, you skip over the constructor call. For example, in the following code, the destructor for x *will* be called, but the constructor won't be:

```
foo()
{
    if( some_condition )
        goto exit;

    some_class  x;   // The constructor is not called. (The goto
                     // branch skips over it.)
    //...
exit:
                     // The destructor for x IS called here, when
}                    // x goes out of scope.
```

Because of this problem, it's best to avoid goto branches altogether in C++ programs.

54.1 Always put a return at the outer level.

Sometimes, when the subroutines are short, it's not worth the trouble to have a single exit point. (To my mind, the "avoid complexity" rule overrides any other rule with which it comes in conflict.) In this situation, always ensure that there are no paths out of the subroutine that don't pass through a return statement. Not this:

```
if( a )
{
    //...
    return doo_wha_ditty();
}
else
{
    //...
    return ERROR;
}
```

but this:

```
if( a )
{
    //...
    return doo_wha_ditty();
}
//...
return ERROR;
```

Ideally, the error return is the outer one so that you correctly handle an unexpected falling through to the outer level.

55. Avoid duplication of effort.

The following code demonstrates the problem:

```
if( strcmp(a, b) < 0 )
{
}
else if ( strcmp(a, b) > 0 )
{
}
else if ( strcmp(a, b) == 0 )
{
}
```

A `strcmp()` call is not low overhead in C (as it is in Pascal and other languages). You're much better off doing:

```
int cmp = strcmp(a,b);
if( cmp < 0 )
{
}
else if (cmp > 0)
{
}
else // cmp == 0
{
}
```

56. Don't corrupt the global name space.

Corruption of the global name space is a particular problem in a team-programming environment. You don't want to be in a position of needing permission from every member of a team every time you introduce a new symbol. So:

- A local variable is always preferable to a class member.
- A class member is always preferable to a static global.
- A static global is always preferable to a true (nonstatic) global.

A `static` global symbol is not exported from the .C file, so it's not visible to other modules. Use `static` for as many global symbols (variables and functions) as possible. A `private` symbol in a class definition is even better. A symbol defined locally within a subroutine is best of all because it's isolated from every other function in the program.

A corollary is: avoid the preprocessor. Because the scope of a macro is so large, it's effectively the same as a global variable.

56.1 Avoid global symbols.

Expanding a bit on the previous rule, two functions are coupled through a global variable when one function sets the global and the other uses it. (If the global wasn't shared, there'd be no reason for it to be global; it could be a `static` local). The coupling relationships associated with globals are particularly nasty maintenance problems because the relationships are difficult to trace. When a global changes at runtime, it's very difficult to find out what changed it. Similarly, if you have to change the behavior of a global object, it's very difficult to find out what uses it. For this reason, it's best to avoid globals altogether. Of course, most real-world programs will need a handful of globals, but as a rule of thumb, I get very nervous if there are more than 10 of them.

You can often limit the scope of a global variable to a single file by declaring it static, which at least limits the damage to a single file. At least you know that all of the coupling relationships are found in the current file. Also bear in mind that everything I've said about global variables also applies to macros, functions, and so forth. You restrict access to functions by making them static if at all possible.

56.2 Never require initialization of a global variable to call a function.

There is one situation where static globals make sense: when you have a system of recursive functions. (You can use static globals to reduce the amount of stack space required by using them to pass values between the subroutines. You never need to use a static global to pass information from one subroutine to another, recursive instance of the same subroutine. A local static variable is the proper choice in this situation. Use static globals in situations where more than one subroutine is invoked: A( ) calls B( ), which calls A( ), which calls B( ), and so forth.)

Because the global variable used by our recursive function is made static to minimize coupling, how do you initialize it? Here's how not to do it. This is file 1:

```
static int glob;

get_glob( x )
{
    return glob;
}

set_glob( x )
{
    glob = x;
}

void recursive_function( void )
{
    int y = glob;
    //...
    recursive_function();
}
```

and here is file 2:

```
set_glob( 10 );
recursive_function();
x = get_glob();
```

You've achieved little here in terms of coupling; in fact, a simple global variable would be easier to manage. Moreover, you've set yourself up for a potential problem: forgetting to call set_glob(). Here's how to do it right:

```
static int glob:

static void recursive_function( void )
{
    int y = glob;
    //...
    recursive_function();
}

int do_recursive( int init_val )
{
    glob = init_val;
    recursive_function();
    return glob;
}
```

Neither the global nor the recursive function can be accessed directly from outside the module because of the static storage class. You must get to the recursive function through the *access function*, do_recursive(), which guarantees that everything is initialized properly before making the call to the recursive function.

50.2.1 Make locals static in recursive functions if the value doesn't span a recursive call

While we're on the subject of recursion, there is a rule to use to reduce stack usage even further. A local variable can be declared static (thereby removing it from the stack) if its value doesn't have to be retained across a recursive call. Here's one example:

```
f()
{
    static int i;
    //...

    for( i = 10; --i >= 0; )
        //...

    f();

    for( i = 10; --i >= 0; )    // i is reinitialized after the
        //...                    // recursive call, so it can be
}                                // static.
```

Here's another:

```
int f()
{
    static int depth     = 0;
    static int depth_max = 0;

    ++depth;
    depth_max = max( depth, depth_max );

    if( depth > 10 )
        return -1;  // recursion level too deep.

    f();

    --depth;
    return depth_max;
}
```

In this last case, the depth variable is used to pass information—the recursion depth—from one instance of the subroutine to another, recursive instance of the same routine. depth_max keeps track of the maximum recursion depth used. depth wouldn't work at all if it had to retain its value across calls—the whole point is that each recursive call modifies the variable.

56.3 Use instance counts in place of initialization functions.

Initialization functions, with the obvious exception of C++ constructors, shouldn't be used simply because it's too easy to forget to call them. Many windowing systems, for example, require you to call a windowing-system-initialization function before creating a window (and another shutdown function after deleting the last window). This is a bad idea. Fix the problem with an instance count, which in C typically needs to be a global variable (declared static to limit its scope). Do it like this:

```
static int num_windows = 0;   // limit access to current module

create_window()
{
    if( ++num_windows == 1 )            // have just created first window
        initialize_video_system();
    //...
}
destroy_window()
{
    //...
    if( --num_windows == 0 )            // have just destroyed last window
        shutdown_video_system();
}
```

You can use a `static` class member for this purpose in C++.

56.4 If an `if` ends in `return`, don't use `else`.

Instead of:

```
if( condition )
    return xxx;
else
{
    do_lots_of_stuff();
}
```

it's usually better to say:

```
if( condition )
    return xxx;

do_lots_of_stuff();
```

It's best to make that last `return` an error return so that you'll get an error back when you inadvertently miss a path.

A conditional statement can also solve the problem in simple situations, and make the code more readable to boot. Rather than:

```
f()
{
    //...
    if( x )
        return 123;
    else if ( y )
        return 456;
    else
        return ERROR;
}
```

use

```
f()
{
    //...
    return x ? 123    :
           y ? 456    :
               ERROR ;
}
```

Note how the formatting makes the foregoing code readable.

One common situation where you have multiple returns looks like this:

```
if( A )
    return FAIL;

else if( B )
    return SUCCESS;

else
{
    // Lots of code
    return SUCCESS;        // Two identical returns statements are suspect
}
```

You can eliminate these as follows. First, eliminate the multiple returns by factoring them to an outer level, like this:

```
if( A )
    return FAIL;

else if( B )
    ;
else
{
    // Lots of code
}
return SUCCESS;
```

Next, get rid of the if clause that has an empty statement attached to it:

```
if( A )
    return FAIL;

else if( !B )
{
    // Lots of code
}
return SUCCESS;
```

57. Put the shortest clause of an if/else on top.

It's often the case that an if/else will have one short clause (usually an error-handling statement) and one large clause that does the work:

```
if( some_error() )
    error( "AAAAghhh!!!!" );
else
{
    // 30 lines of code go here
}
```

Always put the short clause at the top. That is, don't do:

```
if( !some_error() )
{
    // 30 lines of code go here
}
else
    error( "AAAAghhh!!!!" );
```

The problem is that the test in the `if` statement controls the `else` as just as much as it controls the `if`. If the large block comes first, the odds of the `else` being on the next screen or page are quite high. When I've done it wrong, I find myself looking at an `else` and asking "how did I get to here?" If the `if` is visible at the same time, I know how I got there.

58. Try to move errors from run time to compile time.

Uninitialized variables are bugs waiting to happen. You should always initialize a variable when you declare it. In C++, declaration-time initialization is always possible because a declaration can go anywhere a statement can go; just defer the declaration until you have *declaration, can go anywhere* enough information to be able to initialize the variable. This way, you'll get a compile-time error ("variable not found") rather than a runtime error if you try to use the variable prematurely.

In C, you can declare a variable after any open brace, so you can often defer declaration for a while, but you don't have the flexibility of C++. At the very least, initialize the variable to a value that will force the subroutine to blow up in a detectable way if the variable is used; don't let the initial value default to garbage, which might seem like a reasonable value to the code. A pointer initialized to NULL, for example, is safer than one that holds a garbage value that might be a legal address.

On the down side, it's nice to have all of the variable declarations in one place—at the top of a block—so that you can find them easily. If your subroutines are small enough, you can generally do both. For example, you can split up a subroutine to move declarations to the top of a block where you can find them. A subroutine like the following one:

```
f()
{
    // code that doesn't use i

    int i = init_val;
    // code that uses i.
}
```

can be split up as follows:

```
f()
{
    // code that doesn't use i
    g( init_val );
}

g( int init_val )
{
    int i = init_val;
    // code that uses i.
}
```

A general-purpose counter variable that is initialized at the head of a for loop is an obvious exception to this rule. Sometimes the use of too many subroutines can cause more problems than it solves, and an embedded declaration is a better choice. Use your head.

59. Use C function pointers as selectors.

This rule is strictly for C programmers. (C++ programmers should use virtual functions.) In C, replace code like the following:

```c
typedef enum shape_type { CIRCLE, LINE, TEXT };
typedef struct
{
    shape_type type;
    union shape_data
    {   // data here for various shapes.
    }data;

}
shape;

extern void print_circle( shape *p );
extern void print_line  ( shape *p );
extern void print_text  ( shape *p );

shape a_circle = { CIRCLE, ... };

print_shape( shape *p )
{
    switch( p->type )
    {
    case CIRCLE: print_circle( p );
    case LINE:   print_line  ( p );
    case TEXT:   print_text  ( p );
    }
}
```

with:

```
typedef struct
{
    void (*print)( struct *shape );
    union shape_data;
    {   // data here for various shapes.
    }
}
shape;

extern void print_circle( shape *p );
extern void print_line  ( shape *p );
extern void print_text  ( shape *p );

shape a_circle = { print_circle, ... };

print_shape( shape *p )
{
    (p->print)( p );
}
```

The main advantages of this approach are:

- You don't need the shape_type enum any more.
- print_shape() is now much simpler to write.
- print_shape() will continue to work without modification when (not if) you add new shapes to the system.

60. Avoid do/while loops.

A do/while is inherently dangerous because you always execute the body once. Consequently, you have to test termination conditions before entering the loop. I often see code like the following:

```
if( !test_something )
    return ERROR;
do
{
    stuff();

}while( test_something );
```

You're much better off doing:

```
while( test_something )
    stuff();
```

A similar case is:

```
if( some_condition() )
do
    //lots of stuff
while( some_condition() && other_stuff() );
```

which is easily handled with:

```
while( some_condition() )
{
    //lots of stuff
    if( !other_stuff() )
        break;
}
```

I've been programming professionally since 1979 and have used a do/while loop exactly twice in that time.

60.1 Never use a do/while for a forever loop.

Code like the following:

```
do
{
    // several pages of code goes here
while( 1 );
```

just forces the maintenance programmer to flip through your listing looking for the while rather than being able to find it immediately, as would be the case were the while(1) at the top of the loop.

61. Counting loops should count down if possible.

Loops are one of the places where a little efficiency can help program execution quite a bit because the code is executed so many times. Because a test against zero is usually more efficient than one against an explicit number, a loop that counts down is usually more efficient. Use

```
for( i = max; --i >= 0; )
    ;
```

rather than:

```
for( i = 0; i < max; ++i )
    ;
```

Note that, in both cases, the counter can be used as a valid array index, which is something that makes the code less error prone because it tends to keep the array access in bounds.

62. Don't do the same thing in two ways at the same time.

As a counterpoint to the previous rule, consider the following code (which has a bug in it):

```
int array[ARRAY_SIZE];
int *p = array;
for( i = 1; i < ARRAY_SIZE ; ++i )
    *p++ = 0;
```

The problem is that the counter is out of phase with the pointer (i has the value 1 when p points at array[0]), and the last cell won't be initialized.

I generally prefer pointers (instead of array indexes) for simple array traversal because pointers tend to be more efficient, eliminating the multiplication operation implicit in a[i], which is interpreted as:

```
(a + (i* sizeof(a[0])))
```

I'd rewrite this code as follows:

```
int          array[ARRAY_SIZE];
int          *current        = array
int *const end               = array + (SIZE-1);

while( current <= end )
    *current++ = 0;
```

It's equally-safe (though less efficient) to do the following:

```
int array[ARRAY_SIZE];
int i;
for( i = 0; i < ARRAY_SIZE; ++i )
    array[i] = 0;
```

By the way, if you do use pointers, you should derive an index using pointer arithmetic rather than keeping a second variable. You'd have a problem if you passed i to a function in the previous buggy example. Use code like this:

```
for(current = array; current <= end ; ++current)
{
    //
    f( current - array );   // pass f() current array index
}
```

On the other hand, code such as the following should generally be avoided because the loop control is needlessly inefficient:

```
while( (current - array) < ARRAY_SIZE )
    //...
```

63. Use `for` if any two of an initialization, test, or increment are present.

Otherwise, use a while. Code such as:

```
int x = 10;

    // 200 lines of code that don't use x go here

while( x > 0 )
{
    // 200 lines of code go here

    f( x-- );
}
```

is not a great idea, even if you save a marginal amount of time by combining the `--` with the function call. Move the initialization and the x-- into a `for` statement. Because a declaration can go anywhere a statement can go in C++, you can even defer the declaration of x to just above the `for`:

```
int x = 10;
for(; x > 0 ; --x )
{
    // 200 lines of code

    f(x);
}
```

(As an aside, though you can say `for(int x=0;...` in C++, the practice is misleading because the scope of x is actually the outer scope, as if the declaration was on the line preceding the `for`. I don't recommend it.)

If the three statements in a `for` are too long to fit on one line, you can format it like this:

```
for( some_long_variable_name = f();
     some_long_variable_name ;
     some_long_variable_name = f() )
{
    //...
}
```

but it's often better to split out one of the clauses, like this:

```
int some_long_variable_name = ();
for(; some_long_variable_name ; some_long_variable_name = f() )
{
    //...
}
```

or in an extreme case:

```
int    some_extremely_long_variable_name = f();
for(;; some_extremely_long_variable_name = f() )
{
    if( !some_extremely_long_variable_name )
        break;
    //...
}
```

The main point is to get the initialization, test, and increment in one place. I'd never do:

```
int some_extremely_long_variable_name = ();
while( some_extremely_long_variable_name )
{
    // many lines of code

    some_extremely_long_variable_name = f();
}
```

because it breaks up the loop control.

64. If it doesn't appear in the test, it shouldn't appear in the other parts of a `for` statement.

Because the purpose of a `for` statement is to get the initialization, test, and increment parts of a loop into one place so that you can see what's going on with a glance, you don't want to clutter up the `for` statement with stuff that has nothing to do with loop control, or you defeat the whole purpose of the construction. Avoid code like the following:

```
int *ptr;
//...
for( ptr = array, i = array_size; --i >= 0 ; f(ptr++) )
    ;
```

which is better stated as:

```
int *ptr = array;
for( i = array_size; --i >= 0 ; )
    f( ptr++ );
```

65. Assume that things will go wrong.

Some of the best examples of this problem involve "sign extension." Most computers use a form of arithmetic called "twos complement." The most-significant bit of a negative twos-complement number is always 1. For example, an eight-bit signed char holding the number -10 is represented as follows in a twos-complement machine: 11110110 (or 0xf6). The same number in a 16-bit int is represented as 0xfff6. If you convert the 8-bit char to an int, either explicitly with a cast operation or implicitly simply by using it in an arithmetic expression in which the second operand is an int, the compiler coverts the char to an int by adding another byte and duplicating the "sign" bit (the high bit) of the char in every bit of the newly added byte. That's sign extension.

There are two kinds of right-shift operations at the assembly-language level: an "arithmetic shift" gives you sign extension (whatever value was in the high bit before the shift will still be in the high bit after the shift); a "logical shift" fills in from the left with zeros. The rule about whether you get an arithmetic or logical shift when you use the C/C++ shift operator is simple: If you need sign extension, assume that you'll get zero fill. If you need zero fill, assume you'll get sign extension.

Another good example is error-return values. A surprising number of programmers don't bother to check whether malloc() returns NULL if it can't get memory. Maybe they're assuming that there's an infinite amount of virtual memory available, but the fact is that it's easy for a bug to use up all available memory, and you'll never detect the problem if you don't check the error return. If a function can indicate an error condition, you can assume that the error will occur at least once over the life of the program.

66. Computers do not know mathematics.

Computers are arithmetic engines—glorified adding machines. They don't know mathematics. Even expressions as simple as the following one can get you into trouble:

```
int x = 32767;
x = (x * 2) / 2;
```

(x will end up with −1 in it on a 16-bit machine. 32,767 is 0x7fff. The *2 is effectively a left shift by one bit, yielding 0xfffe—a negative number. The /2 is an arithmetic right shift; sign extension is guaranteed, so you now have 0xffff or −1.) It's important to consider the limitations of the hardware every time you do arithmetic. If you multiply before dividing, you run the risk of running out of bits to store the number; if you divide first, you run the risk of truncating to zero; and so forth. Entire books have been written on numerical analysis for computers, and you should read at least one of these if you do a lot of math in your programs.

You also have to know the peccadillos of your language. In C, for example, type conversions are done on an operator-by-operator basis. I once spent a morning trying to figure out why the following code didn't do anything:

```
long x;
x &= 0xffff; // clear all but the bottom 16 bits of a 32-bit long.
```

The machine had a 16-bit int and a 32-bit long. The constant 0xffff is an int with the arithmetic value −1. The C compiler, when processing the &=, saw dissimilar operand types, so converted the int to a long. A −1 represented as as a long is 0xffffffff, so the AND operation has no effect. This is the way the language is supposed to work. I just didn't think.

Note that you *cannot* fix this problem with a cast. All that the following code does is make the implicit type conversion explicit. The same type conversion happens, however:

```
x &= (long)0xffff;
```

The only way to fix the problem is with:

```
x &= 0xffffUL;
```

or equivalent.

66.1 Expect the impossible.

A switch should always have a default case, especially if the default shouldn't happen:

```
f( int i )   // i should have the value 1 or 2.
{
    switch( i )
    {
    case 1: do_something();          break;
    case 2: do_something_else();     break;

    default:
            fprintf(stderr,
                "Internal error in f(): illegal value of i (%d)", i );
            exit( -1 );
    }
}
```

The same goes for if/else blocks that work in a switch-like fashion.

A loop should also test for the impossible. The following code works even if i is initially zero—something that's not supposed to happen:

```
f( int i )   // i should be positive
{
    while( --i >= 0 )
        do_something();
}
```

A while(--i) is less robust because it fails miserably when i is initially zero.

66.2 Always check error-return codes.

This should be self evident, but the ISO/ANSI C++ committee required new to throw an exception when it couldn't get memory because it discovered that some ridiculous number of runtime errors in real programs were caused by people not bothering to check whether new evaluated to NULL.

I've also seen a lot of code in which people didn't bother to see if fopen() actually worked before they started using the FILE pointer.

67. Avoid explicit temporary variables.

Most variables that are used only once fall into this category. For example:

```
int x = *p++;
f( x );
```

should be:

```
f( *p++ );
```

Rarely, an explicit temporary is useful when you need to guarantee order of evaluation or if an expression is simply so long that it's unreadable. In the latter case, the variable name is providing useful documentation and, if chosen properly, can eliminate the need for a comment. For example, you can replace:

```
f( Coefficient_of_lift * (0.5 * RHO * square(v)) ); // pass f() the generated lift
```

with:

```
double lift = Coefficient_of_lift * (0.5 * RHO * square(v));
f( lift );
```

This rule is not prohibiting either of these uses, but rather the degenerate use I mentioned first.

68. No magic numbers.

The main body of your code should not have explicit numbers in it. Use enum or const to give the number a symbolic name. (I've discussed elsewhere why a **#define** isn't a great choice here.) There are two advantages:

- The symbolic name makes the value self documenting, obviating the need for a comment.
- If the number is used in more than one place, there's only one thing to change—the constant definition.

I sometimes make an exception to this rule for locally used variables. For example, the following code uses a magic number (128):

```
f()
{
    char buf[128];
    ...
    fgets( buf, sizeof(buf)/sizeof(*buf), stdin );
}
```

Because I've used sizeof() in the fgets() call, changes made to the array size are automatically reflected in the code. Adding an extra symbol to hold the size would add unnecessary complexity.

69. Make no assumptions about sizes.

The classic problem is code that assumes that an `int` is 32 bits. The following code doesn't work if you have a 32-bit pointer and a 16-bit `int` (as you can on the 80x86):

```
double   a[1000], *p = a;
//...
dist_from_start_of_array_in_bytes = (int)p - (int)a;
```

A more subtle problem in C (but not C++) is:

```
g()
{
    doesnt_work( 0 );
}

doesnt_work( char *p )
{
    if( !p )      // probably doesn't work
        //...
}
```

The compiler accepts the call because forward references are permitted in C. (They aren't in C++ so the foregoing isn't a problem in C++.) 0 is an `int`, so a 16-bit object is pushed on the stack, The function expects a (32-bit) pointer however, so it uses the 16 bits that were pushed and adds another 16 bits of garbage to make the 32-bit pointer. Odds are the `if(!p)` will fail because only 16 of the 32 bits will be zero.

A traditional solution is to use typedefs:

```
typedef int    word;       // always 16 bits
typedef long   dword;      // always 32 bits.
```

You can then change the `typedef` statements in a new environment to assure that a `word` remains 16 bits and a `dword` remains 32 bits. A 32-bit system might redefine the foregoing as:

```
typedef short  word;       // always 16 bits
typedef int    dword;      // always 32 bits.
```

Another size-related time bomb is hidden in the way that ANSI C does internationalization. ANSI C defines the `wchar_t` type to handle wide character sets such as Unicode—the new 16-bit multinational character set. The ANSI C standard also says that wide-character string constants should be preceded by an `L`. Microsoft and other compiler vendors try to help you write portable code by providing macros like the following:

```
#ifdef _UNICODE
    typedef wchar_t _TCHAR
#   define _T(x) L##x
#else
    typedef char _TCHAR
#   define _T(x) x
#endif
```

If `_UNICODE` is not defined, the statement:

```
_TCHAR *p = _T("doo wha ditty");
```

evaluates to:

```
char *p = "doo wha ditty";
```

If _UNICODE is defined, the same statement evaluates to:

```
wchar_t *p = L"doo wha ditty";
```

So far, so good. You might now try to move your existing code into a Unicode environment simply by using your editor to replace all instances of char with _TCHAR and replace all string constants with the original text, bracketed with _T(and). The problem is that code such as the following (in which the _TCHAR was originally a char) no longer works:

```
_TCHAR str[4];
//...
int max_chars = sizeof(str); // assumes 1-byte char
```

A _TCHAR will be two-bytes wide when _UNICODE is defined, so your character count will be twice the actual number of characters in the string. You'd have to use the following to fix the problem:

```
int max_chars = sizeof(str) / sizeof(*str) ;
```

70. Beware of casts (C issues).

The cast operator is often misunderstood. A cast *does not* tell the compiler to "treat this variable as if it were declared as this type." It should be viewed as a *runtime* operation that creates a temporary variable of the type specified in the cast, then initializes the temporary variable from the operand. In C++, of course, this initialization can be very-high overhead because a constructor can be called.

The first place that a misunderstanding of a cast can get you into trouble is in C, where function prototypes aren't required. When a compiler sees a function call without a preceding prototype, the compiler assumes that the function returns an int. The following code *does not* say "malloc() actually returns a pointer, not an int":

```
int *p  = (int *) malloc( sizeof(int) );
```

rather, the code says "I assume that malloc() returns an int because there's no preceding prototype, convert that int to a pointer to assign it to p). If an int is 16 bits and a pointer is 32 bits, you're now in deep doo doo. The malloc() call might well return a 32-bit pointer, but because the compiler assumes that malloc() returns a 16-bit int, it ignores the other 16 bits. The compiler then takes the truncated 16-bit quantity and converts it to a 32-bit int as best as it is able, usually by filling in the top 16 bits with zeros. If the pointer happened to hold an address greater than 0xffff, which is likely on most machines, you've just lost the high bits. The only way to fix this problem is by preceding the malloc() call with a proper prototype that says that malloc() returns a pointer (usually by including <stdlib.h>).

The next issue is that the foregoing cast might have been put into the code just to shut up the compiler, which will most certainly generate a type-mismatch warning if the cast is missing. Casts are often abused in this way—to shut up the compiler when you should really be paying attention to the warning. Many compilers, for example, generate a warning about possible truncation when given the following code:

```
f( int x );

//...

unsigned y;
f( y );
```

and many programmers will shut up the compiler with an `f((int)y)`. The cast, though, doesn't change the fact that an `unsigned int` can hold a value that won't fit into a signed `int`, so the resulting call might not work.

Here's a similar problem that comes up with function pointers. The following code happens to work fine:

```
some_object array[ size ];
int my_cmp( some_object *p1, some_object *p2 );

qsort( array, size, sizeof(some_object), ((*)(void*,void*)) my_cmp ),
```

The similar code that follows fails miserably with no warning messages:

```
some_object array[ size ];
void foo( int x );

qsort( array, size, sizeof(some_object), ((*)(void*,void*)) foo );
```

`qsort()` passes pointer arguments to `foo()`, but `foo()` expects an `int` argument, so it will use an `int`'s worth of the pointer. Worse, `foo()` will return a garbage value, which `qsort()` will use because it expects an `int` return value.

Alignment presents difficulties as well. Many machines require objects of certain types to be at specific addresses. For example, though a one-byte `char` can be placed at any address in memory, a two-byte `short` might have to be at an even address, and a four-byte `long` might have to be at an address that's an even multiple of four. The following code, again, generates no warnings but can cause the program to blow up at runtime:

```
short x;
long  *lp = (long*)( &x );
*lp = 0;
```

This bug is particularly nasty, because the `*lp=0` fails only if x happens to be at an address that is not an even multiple of four. The code might seem to work until you add a declaration for another `short` just above x, then the program blows up.

One compiler that I know of tries to deal with this problem by actually modifying the contents of the pointer to guarantee a legal address as a side effect of the cast. In other words, the following code could actually modify p:

```
p = (char *)(long *)p;
```

71. Handle special cases directly.

Write your algorithms in such a way that they'll handle the degenerate cases directly. Here's a trivial example of the wrong way to do things:

```
print( const char *str )
{
    if( !*str )        // nothing to do, string is empty
        return;

    while( *str )
        putchar( *str++ );
}
```

The if statement is unnecessary because this case is handled quite well by the while loop.

Listings 2 and 3 demonstrate a more realistic scenario. Listing 2 defines a deliberately naive doubly-linked-list header and a function to remove an element.

Listing 2. Linked list: Case 1.

```
 1  typedef struct node
 2  {
 3      struct node *next, *prev;
 4      //...
 5  } node;
 6
 7  node *head;
 8
 9  remove( node **headp, node *remove )
10  {
11      // Remove the node pointed to by "remove" from the list whose
12      // head is at *headp.
13
14      if( *headp == remove )      // The node is at the head of the list.
15      {
16          if( remove->next )              // If it's not the only node in
17              remove->next->prev = NULL;  // the list, position the
18                                          // successor at the first node.
19          *headp = remove->next;
20      }
21      else                        // The node is in the middle of the list
22      {
23          remove->prev->next = remove->next;
24          if( remove->next )
25              remove->next->prev = remove->prev;
26      }
27  }
```

Listing 3 shows code that does the same thing, but I've modified the previous-node pointer in the node structure by making it hold the address of the previous node's next field rather than a holding pointer to the entire structure. This simple change means that the first element is no longer a special case, so the remove function becomes dramatically simpler.

The point is that a slight recasting of the problem allows me to use an algorithm that doesn't have special cases, thereby simplifying the code. Of course, this simplicity doesn't come for free—it's now impossible to traverse backwards through the list—but we might not need that capability.

Listing 3. Linked list: Case 2.

```
 1   typedef struct node
 2   {
 3       struct node *next, **prev;  // <=== Added a * to prev
 4       //...
 5   } node;
 6
 7   node *head;
 8
 9   remove( node **headp, node *remove )
10   {
11       if( *(remove->prev) = remove->next )      // if not at end of list
12           remove->next->prev = remove->prev ;   // adjust successor
13   }
```

72. Don't try to make lint happy.

Lint is a C syntax checker. (There's also a C++ version available in the MS-DOS/Windows world. It's manufactured by Gimple Software.) Though these programs are invaluable for occasional use, they print out so many garbage error messages and warnings that your code will be almost impossible to read if you get rid of all of them. Code like the following should be avoided:

```
(void) printf("...");
```

There's nothing at all wrong with assignment in a loop:

```
while( p = f() )
    g(p);
```

even if a novice programmer might use = instead of ==. (The problems of novices should not matter when you're considering style guidelines for experienced professionals. It's like passing a law that says that all bicycles must have training wheels because 2-year-olds have a hard time riding without them.)

I've read a suggestion that you can have the compiler find inadvertant assignment (when you actually meant to compare) simply by putting constant values first. For example, the following code would give you a compiler error if you used = instead of ==:

```
#define MAX 100
//...
if( MAX == x )
    //...
```

The idea has some merit, but I find the code somewhat hard to read.

73. Put memory allocation and deallocation code in the same place.

Memory leaks—allocating memory but forgetting to free it—are a big problem in applications that have to run for any length of time: database servers, point-of-sale software, operating systems, and so forth. There are lots of ways to track the problem. Many programs, for example, modify `malloc()` to keep an "in-use" list that can be traversed by `free()` to see if the pointer is valid. You can also augment the header needed for in-use-list maintenance by storing information about where the allocation occurred. (Pass __LINE__ and __FILE__ into your debugging malloc().) The in-use list should be empty when the program exits. If it isn't, you can traverse the list and, at least, find out from where the memory came.

Detection is desirable, but prevention is better. If possible, you should put a free() in the same function as the matching malloc(). For example, use this:

```
void user( void )
{
    p = malloc( size );
    producer( p );
    consumer( p );
    free( p );
}
```

instead of this:

```
void *producer( )
{
    void *p = malloc( size );
    //...
    return p;
}
void consumer( void *p )
{
    //...
    free( p );
}
void user( void )
{
    void *p = producer();
    consumer( p );
}
```

You can't always do the foregoing in C, however. For example, the earlier rules about uninitialized variables applies to memory from malloc(), too. It's better to do this:

```
some_object *p = allocate_and_init(); // Does not return if no
                                       // memory is available.
```

than to do this:

```
some_object *p = malloc( sizeof(some_object) );
if( !p )
    fatal_error("Out of memory!");
init();
```

C++ solves this problem with constructors.

74. Heap memory is expensive.

The other main malloc()/free() (or new/delete) issue is the time required to do memory management, which can be significant. I've reduced run times by as much as 50% by replacing multiple calls to malloc() and free() with other strategies. For example, if you have a very-active data structure of identical objects, you can use something like the code in Listing 4 to manage data-structure members.

Listing 4. Managing your own free list.

```
1    typedef struct some_class
2    {
3        struct some_class *next;
4        //...
5    }
6    some_class ;
7
8    static some_class *free_list = NULL;
9    //--------------------------------------------------------------
10   free_object( some_class *object )
11   {
12       // Rather than passing the memory to free() link it onto
13       // the head of a free list.
14
15       object->next = free_list;
16       free_list = object;
17   }
18   //--------------------------------------------------------------
19   free_all_objects( )
20   {
21       // Free up all of the objects on the free list. Sorting the
22       // objects by base address before entering the loop will
23       // improve free's performance, but I'm not doing that here.
24       // (Quicksort lends itself to linked-list sorting nicely.)
25
26       some_object *current;
27       while( free_list )
28       {
29           current = free_list;
30           free_list = current->next;
31           free( current );
32       }
33   }
34   //--------------------------------------------------------------
35   some_class *new_object( )
36   {
37       // If there's an object on the free list, use it. Get an
38       // object from malloc() only if the free list is empty.
39
40       some_class *object;
41       if( free_list )
42       {
43           object = free_list;            // unlink from list
44           free_list = object->next;
45       }
46       else
47       {
48           // You could improve performance further by allocating
49           // objects in blocks of 100 rather than one at a time,
50           // but that also complicates the free_all_objects()
51           // function.
52
```

➡

Listing 4. continued. . .
```
53            object = malloc( sizeof(some_class) );
54      }
55
56      if( object )
57            // put initialization code here
58
59      return object;
60   }
```

75. Test routines should not be interactive.

I am often presented with test functions that have elaborate interactive user interfaces. Not only is this a waste of time, it doesn't make for very complete testing. People sitting at keyboards trying whatever comes into their heads are not exactly systematic. It's better for a noninteractive test function to systematically exercise those functions that need to be tested.

Don't ever erase that test subroutine, by the way; just use an `#ifdef` TEST to include or exclude the routine from your compile. If you're like me, you'll erase the test function in the morning and need it again that afternoon, even if you haven't used it in the past two years.

76. An error message should tell the user what's right.

Back in the days of CP/M, the DDT debugger had a single error message. No matter what you did wrong, it said:

```
?
```

Though error handling like this fortunately is no longer the norm, I still see it, albeit with fancier trappings. Several Windows programs that I own just ring the bell when I enter an invalid item into a dialog box, leaving me to wonder what a valid item is. I've often seen error messages that gave me copious amounts of information about what I did wrong, but don't give me a clue about how to do it right. In the most frustrating situation, a dialog prompts you to enter a number, but when you enter the wrong number, it prints a message like:

```
Invalid value.
```

without a clue about what a valid value might be. Sometimes the dialog refuses to shut down unless you enter a valid value. Sometimes the program is in control of the machine, and you can't switch to another application to terminate the one that's giving you grief. (Windows calls this "feature" a system-modal dialog box. Please don't use these). So there you are, faced with the choice of terminating the program with a Ctrl-C or equivalent (if you can), turning off the power, or randomly typing in numbers until you happen to hit on one that the data-entry code is happy with. The question is whether it will take more time to redo the last three hours' work, which you didn't think of saving before you brought up the dialog, or to spend the next three hours playing 20 questions with a dialog box. It's this sort of thing that gives computers a bad name.

An error message should tell you how to fix the problem, something like:

```
Numbers must be in the range 17 to 63, inclusive.
```

or:

```
Dates must take the form mm-dd-yyyy.
```

There should be some way (like a "help" button) to get more information if you need it. Finally, you must have a way to harmlessly terminate the data-entry process (like a "Cancel" button).

77. Don't print error messages if an error is recoverable.

Library routines (and most low-level subroutines) should not print error messages. They should return an error code that can be tested by the caller. This way the caller can take some remedial action. For example, if a recursive quick-sort function prints an error when it runs out of stack, the calling subroutine can't retry the sort using a different, nonrecursive algorithm. The user would be looking at the error message even if the second sort attempt succeeds.

78. Don't use system-dependent functions for error messages.

Many window-based environments don't support a notion of standard output or error. (In these environments `printf()` or `fprintf(stderr,...)` calls are typically ignored.) If you make assumptions about your environment, you'll find yourself needing to make massive changes just to get a recompile to work in a new environment.

At minimum, protect yourself like this:

```
#define error        printf
#define terminate(x) ExitProcess(x)
```

then use:

```
if( some_error )
{
    error( "Something's wrong here " );
    terminate( -1 );
}
```

Here's a more flexible solution:

```
#include <stdio.h>
#include <stdarg.h>

#ifdef WINDOWS
    void error( const char* format, ... )
    {
        char buf[255]; // hope it's big enough

        va_list args;
        va_start( args, format );
        if( vsprintf(buf, format, args ) < sizeof(buf) )
            ::MessageBox(NULL, buf, "*** ERROR ***", MB_OK | MB_ICONEXCLAMATION );
        else
        {
            ::MessageBox(NULL,   "Buffer overflow while printing error message.",
                                 "Fatal Error",
                                 MB_OK | MB_ICONEXCLAMATION );
            ExitProcess( -1 );
        }
        va_end( args );
    }
#elif MOTIF
    // Motif-specific error function goes here
#else
    void error( const char* format, ... )
    {
        va_list args;
        va_start( args, format );
        vfprintf(stderr, format, args );
        va_end  ( args );
    }
#endif
```

The Preprocessor

Many features of C++ make the C preprocessor less important than it traditionally has been. Nonetheless, there are times when the preprocessor is needed even in a C++ program, and of course the preprocessor is still an essential part of C programming. Rules in this part of the book concern themselves with proper use of the preprocessor.

I should say that a lot of macros I've seen are on rather shaky ground when it comes to readability and maintenance. I will often not use a macro if an equivalent function will do the same job in a more readable fashion, and I will never use a macro that has side effects (discussed below). In C++ I *never* use parameterized macros, using `inline` functions or templates that expand to inline functions instead. A parameterized macro, even in C, should be a method of last resort. They are hard to debug (because you can't trace into them), often hard to read, and difficult to maintain at best. Use them only when execution speed is a real issue, verified by actually testing the code. This part of the book, then, contains rules for those situations where the preprocessor is the only solution to a problem.

79. Everything in a .h file should be used in at least two .c files.

This rule is pretty self explanatory—don't clutter the global name space with symbols that aren't used globally. If a symbol isn't used outside of the current file, it should be declared only in the scope of the current file. If this unshared symbol is a global variable or function, it should be declared `static`.

Note that `static` functions have their place even in C++. There's a tendency to put all workhorse functions used by any of the message handlers into the class definition itself. Sometimes a local `static` function in the *.cpp* file does the job just as well, and the prototype for the function need not clutter up the class definition.

80. Use nested `#include`s.

Though most of the rules in this part tell you how to avoid the preprocessor, the `#include` mechanism is an indispensable preprocessor function in both C an C++. Nonetheless, there are problems even here.

It's a really bad idea to require someone to `#include` one file to be able to `#include` another. I'm always getting the includes out of sequence or forgetting one of them. Consequently, a *.h* file should always `#include` those files that define things that are used in the current *.h* file. Because problems can arise if the compiler reads a *.h* file more than once, you must take steps to prevent multiple processing of the same file. Put lines like:

```
#ifndef FILENAME_H__
#define FILENAME_H__
```

at the top of every *.h* file, and put a matching:

```
#endif // FILENAME_H__
```

at the bottom. Because `FILENAME_H__` is defined the second time the preprocessor processes the file, the contents are ignored on the second pass.

81. You should always be able to replace a macro with a function.

This is the macro version of the "no surprises" rule. Something that looks like a function should act like one, even if it's really a macro. (For this reason, I will sometimes not fully capitalize the macro name if it's behavior is sufficiently function like. I'll always use all caps if the macro has side effects, though). There are several issues.

First, a macro shouldn't use a variable that's not passed in as an argument. Here's the worst possible way to do things:

The following code is in a *.h* file:

```
#define end()  while(*p) \
                      ++p
```

and the following is in a *.c* file:

```
char *f( char *str )
{
    char *p = str;
    end();
    //...
    return p;
}
```

There are several nasty surprises for the maintenance programmer here. First, the variable p is apparently unused, so there's a temptation to delete it, thereby breaking the code. Similarly the code breaks if the name p is changed to something else. Finally, it's really surprising that calling end(), which looks like a normal function call, would modify p.

A first attempt to fix the problem might look like the following. In the .h file:

```
#define end(p)  while(*p) \
                      ++p
```

and in the .c file:

```
char *f( char *str )
{
    end(str);
    //...
    return str;
}
```

But now, the macro still surprisingly modifies str—a normal C function couldn't work like this. (A C++ function could, but it shouldn't. I'll explain why in the C++ part of the book.) To modify str in a function, you'd have to pass in its address, so the same should apply to the macro. Here's a third (finally correct) variant in which the end() macro is easily replaced by a similarly named function. In the .h file:

```
#define end(p)  while(*(*p)) \
                      ++(*p)
```

and in a .c file:

```
char *f( char *str )
{
    end(&str);
    //...
    return str;
}
```

The end(&str) expands to:

```
while(*(*&p))
    ++(*&p)
```

and *&p is the same as p—the * and & cancel each other—so the macro effectively does the following:

```
while(*(p))
    ++(p)
```

The second macro-as-function problem occurs when you want to do more than one thing in the macro. Consider this macro:

```
#define two_things()      a();b()

if( x )
    two_things();
else
    something_else();
```

which expands as follows (I've reformatted to make what's going on painfully obvious):

```
if( x )
    a();
b();
else
    something_else();
```

You get a "no preceding if for else" error message. You cannot solve the problem with curly braces alone. Redefining two_things to:

```
#define two_things { a(); b(); }
```

causes this expansion:

```
if( x )
{
    a();
    b();
}
;
else
    something_else();
```

That troublesome semicolon was the one that followed the two_things() in the macro invocation. Remember, a semicolon by itself is a legal statement in C. It doesn't do anything, but it's legal. Consequently, the else tries to bind to the semicolon, and you get the same "no preceding if for else."

It's unreasonable to say that, even though this macro looks like a function call, its invocation may not be followed by a semicolon. Fortunately, there are two real solutions to this problem. The first uses the little-known "sequence" (or comma) operator:

```
#define two_things()      (a(),b())
```

This comma is the comma that separates subexpressions in the initialization or increment part of a for statement. (The comma that separates function arguments is not the sequence operator.) The sequence operator evaluates left to right and evaluates to the rightmost thing in the list (here to whatever b() returns). Saying:

```
x = (a(),b());
```

is just like saying:

```
a();
x = b();
```

If you didn't care what the macro evaluated to, you could do a similar thing using a plus sign instead of a comma. (The statement:

```
a()+b();
```

alone on a line is perfectly legal C, there's no requirement that the result of the addition be stored anywhere.) The order of evaluation wouldn't be guaranteed with a plus sign, however; b() might be called first. (Don't confuse associativity rules with order of evaluation. Associativity just tells the compiler where to put implicit parentheses. Order of evaluation takes over once all of the parentheses are in place. There's no way to add additional parentheses to ((a())+(b())).) The sequence operator is guaranteed to evaluate left to right, so it doesn't have these problems.

I should also point out that the sequence operator is bordering on too weird to appear in normal code. I only use it in macros, and then I provide copious comments explaining what's going on. Never use a comma when a semicolon will do the job. (I've seen people do this to avoid using braces, but that's too ugly for words.)

The second solution uses braces, but with a twist:

```
#define two_things()    \
        do              \
        {               \
            a();        \
            b();        \
        } while( 0 )

if( x )
    two_things();
else
    something_else();
```

which expands to:

```
if( x )
    do
    {
        a();
        b();
    } while( 0 ) ; // <== semicolon binds to the while(0)
else
    something_else();
```

You can also use:

```
#define two_things()    \
        if( 1 )         \
        {               \
            a();        \
            b();        \
        } else
```

but I think the do/while(0) is marginally cleaner.

Because you can declare a variable following any open brace, you can use the foregoing technique to define a macro that effectively has its own local variables. Consider the following macro, which swaps two ints:

```
#define swap_int(x,y)    \
        do               \
        {                \
            int x##y;    \
            x##y = x;    \
            x    = y;    \
            y    = x##y  \
        }                \
        while(0)
```

The **##** is the ANSI C concatenation operator. I'm using it here to assure that the temporary-variable name doesn't conflict with either input-variable name. Given the invocation:

```
swap(laurel,hardy);
```

the preprocessor first substitutes arguments in the normal way (replacing x with `laurel` and y with `hardy`), yielding the following for the temporary-variable name:

```
int laurel##hardy;
```

The preprocessor then removes the hash marks, yielding:

```
int laurelhardy;
```

One added benefit of being able to replace macros with functions is debugging. Sometimes you want something to be a macro for efficiency, but you need to set a breakpoint at it when debugging. Use `inline` functions for this in C++, and use the following in C:

```
#define _AT_LEFT(this)    ((this)->left_child_is_thread ? NULL : (this)->left)

#ifdef DEBUG
    static tnode *at_left(tnode *this){ return _AT_LEFT(this);   }
#else
#   define at_left(this)   _AT_LEFT(this)
#endif
```

I'll finish up this rule by mentioning two more weird constructions that are occasionally useful in a macro, primarily because it's helpful for a macro to expand to a single statement to avoid the brace issues discussed earlier. That is, you want the macro to expand to a single expression if possible. The comma operator accomplishes this at the cost of readability, and as with the comma operator, I *never* use the forms shown in Table 1 in normal code for the same reason—they're too hard to read. (For that matter, I don't even use them in macros if I can come up with some other way to do it.)

The first two expressions count on the fact that evaluation of an expression using && or || is guaranteed to go from left to right, and evaluation terminates as soon as truth or falsity can be determined. Taking a && f() as an example. If a is false, then it doesn't matter what f() returns because the expression will evaluate false if either operand is false. Consequently, the compiler never calls f() if a is false, but it must call f() when a is true. The same applies in reverse to b; f() is called only if b is false.

Table 1. Macro equivalents to `if` statements.

This code:	Does the same thing as:
`(a && f())`	`if( a )` `    f();`
`(b || f())`	`if( !b )` `    f();`

`(z ? f() : g())`	`if( z )`
	`    f();`
	`else`
	`    g();`

81.1 `?:` **is not the same as** `if`/`else`.

The last entry in Table 1 brings up another issue. The conditional operator is just that, an operator. It occurs only in an expression, and it evaluates to a value. The conditional operator is not usually a replacement for an `if`/`else` statement, any more than `&&` or `||` are reasonable replacements for a simple `if`. Though most people wouldn't consider replacing:

```
if( z )
    i = j;
else
    i = k;
```

with:

```
z && (i = j);
z || (i.= k);
```

I've occasionally seen the equivalent done with a conditional:

```
z ? (i = j) : (i = k) ;
```

All of the foregoing code is equally wrongheaded. The following code shows the proper way to use a conditional operator, and the result is cleaner (i.e. better) than an equivalent `if`/`else`:

```
i = z ? j : k ;
```

81.2 Parenthesize macro bodies and arguments.

This rule is pretty basic, but I've found that a lot of people who use C on a daily basis have forgotten it. Here's the classic problem:

```
#define TWO_K  1024 + 1024
```

which when used in:

```
10 * TWO_K
```

expands to:

```
10 * 1024 + 1024
```

which evaluates to:

```
(10 * 1024) + 1024
```

Solve the problem with parentheses:

```
#define TWO_K   (1024 + 1024)
```

There's a similar problem in the following code:

```
#define SQUARE(x) (x * x)
```

Given:

```
SQUARE(y + 1);
```

the macro expands to:

```
y + 1 * y + 1
```

and evaluates to:

```
y + (1 * y) + 1
```

Again, parentheses come to the rescue. The following definition:

```
#define SQUARE(x) ((x) * (x))
```

expands to:

```
((y + 1) * (y + 1))
```

82. `enum` and `const` are better than a macro.

A `#define` should be your last choice when defining a constant value. Consider the following common bug discussed earlier:

```
#define TWO_K   1024 + 1024

x = TWO_K * 10
```

which evaluates to 11,264 (1024+(1024*10)) rather than the desired 20,480. An `enum` definition like:

```
enum { two_k = 1024 + 1024 };
```

or a `const` like:

```
const int Two_k = 1024 + 1024;
```

have none of the problems of the macro. Parentheses aren't required.

The `enum` has several points in its favor over a `const`: First, the `const int` definition *in C* actually allocates space for the `int` and initializes that space. You can't modify the space, but it does take up some memory. Consequently, a C `const` definition can't go in a *.h* file; you need an `extern` as you would with any other global variable. (None of this is a factor in C++, which allocates space only if you take the address of the `const` or pass it by reference. C++ `const` definitions can—in fact, often should—go into a *.h* file.)

The `enum` is different in that space is never allocated for it. Like a macro, it can be evaluated at compile time. Consequently, there's no performance loss when you use an `enum`.

The second issue is corruption of the global name space. The scope of an `enum` is easily limited. For example, in the following code, `default_i` is visible only inside the function `f()`:

```
void f( int i )
{
    enum { default_i = 1024 };

    if( !i )
        i = default_i ;
}
```

In:

```
void f( int i )
{
    #define DEFAULT_I 1024

    if( !i )
        i = DEFAULT_I ;
}
```

DEFAULT_I is visible to all functions whose definitions follow the macro definition. If DEFAULT_I were defined in a .h file, it could be visible in several files—even if the code in those files didn't use it. The same problem applies even to a const defined at the global level.

The enum is particularly useful in C++ because it can be limited to class scope and initialized in the class definition itself rather than the constructor. These issues are discussed further in the C++-rules part of the book.

Finally, an enum can be used as the argument to a case statement and as the array size in an array declaration. A const can't be used in either situation.

83. A parameterized-macro argument should not appear more than once on the right-hand side.

The SQUARE() macro presented above has a serious problem even in it's modified form. Given:

```
#define SQUARE(x) ((x)*(x))
```

The statement SQUARE(++x) increments x twice. The macro also evaluates incorrectly in this case. If x starts out holding 2, SQUARE(++x) effectively evaluates to 3 * 4. This behavior is an example of a macro *side effect*—a situation where the macro behaves unexpectedly.

SQUARE(++x) is also an example of a situation where using a macro is simply too risky to justify the maintenance difficulties. A C++ inline function, or a template that expands to an inline function, is a much better solution. Even in C, a simple function with worst-case arguments is more maintainable than the equivalent macro:

```
double square( double x )
{
    return x * x;
}
```

There's considerable doubt in my mind that it's worth using a function to hide a simple multiplication, however.

83.1 Never use macros for character constants.

For example:

```
#define SPACE ' '
```

makes sense only if you are going to use a character other than space in place of a space (as when you're testing a tab-expansion program, for example).

Never do this:

```
#define SPACE 0x20
```

The actual value of the character constant for a space (' ') is changed by the compiler to suit the compilation environment. It is 0x20 in an ASCII environment and something else in an EBCDIC environment. Don't assume that any character has a particular value.

84. When all else fails, use the preprocessor.

We'll see in the C++ part of the book that that the C preprocessor doesn't have much place in C++. There are a few places where it's still handy, though. The first is:

```
#ifdef DEBUG
#    define D(x) x
#else
#    define D(x) /* empty */
#endif
```

The D() macro expands to its argument if you're debugging, otherwise it expands to an empty string. It's used like this:

```
f()
{
    D( printf("Here's a debugging diagnostic\n"); )
}
```

In this case, the argument to D() is the entire printf() statement, which will disappear when you're not debugging.

Another similar use is handy when you have to initialize those inevitable few globals in a large program. The problem is keeping the variable declarations (in a *.h* file) in synch with the variable definitions (in a *.c* file), where space is actually allocated and the variable is initialized. Here's a sample *.h* file:

```
#ifdef ALLOC
#    define   I(x)        x
#    define   EXPORTED    /*empty*/
#else
#    define   I(x)        /*empty*/
#    define   EXPORTED    extern
#endif

EXPORTED int           glob_x[10] I( ={1, 2, 3, 4} );
EXPORTED some_object   glob_y     I( ("constructor", "arguments")  );
```

In exactly one place in your program (I typically do it in a file called *globals.cpp*), you'll put the lines:

```
#define ALLOC
#include "globals.h"
```

Everywhere else, you'll just include the file without the previous **#define** ALLOC. When you compile *globals.cpp*, the **#define** ALLOC forces the following expansion:

```
/*empty*/ int            glob_x[10] ={1, 2, 3, 4};
/*empty*/ some_object    glob_y       ("constructor", "arguments");
```

Everywhere else, the lack of a **#define** ALLOC forces the following expansion:

```
extern int            glob_x[10] /*empty*/ ;
extern some_object    glob_y     /*empty*/ ;
```

The final example of preprocessor usage is the ASSERT() macro, which prints an error message and terminates the program only when you are debugging (DEBUG is **#defined**) and the argument to ASSERT() is false. It's very useful for testing things like NULL pointer arguments. One version of ASSERT(), which is used like this:

```
f( char *p )
{
    ASSERT( p, "f(): Unexpected NULL arg." );
}
```

is defined as follows:

```
#ifdef DEBUG
    #define ASSERT(condition,msg)
            if( !(condition) ) \
            {\
              fprintf(stderr,"ASSERT(" #condition ") FAILED "\
                            "[File " __FILE__ ", Line %d]:\n\t%s\n",\
                            __LINE__, (msg) );\
              exit( -1 );\
            }\
            else
#else
#   define ASSERT(c,m) /* empty */
#endif
```

In the earlier example, the ASSERT() prints the following string when the assertion fails:

```
ASSERT(p) FAILED [File whatever.cpp, Line 123]:
    f(): Unexpected NULL arg.
```

then exits the program. It gets the current file name and line number from the preprocessor using the predefined __FILE__ and __LINE__ macros. The condition that causes the failure is printed using the ANSI C "stringization" operator (the **#**), which effectively surrounds the expanded argument with quote marks after doing the argument substitution. (The #condition expands to "p" in the current example.) Then normal C string concatenation comes into play to merge together the various strings, creating a single format argument to fprintf().

You have to use the preprocessor here, because you need to print the file and line number on which the assertion was made. A C++ inline function could only print the file and line number in which the `inline` function was defined.

All ANSI C compilers should implement an `assert(expr)` macro in *assert.h*, but the ANSI C macro has no ability to print a custom error message. An ANSI C `assert()` is enabled when NDEBUG is not defined (the default).

C-Related Rules

This section discusses the C-specific programming rules that weren't covered in the previous sections.

85. Stamp out the demons of complexity (Part 2).

The complexity demons are particularly nasty in C. The language itself seems to encourage unnaturally complicated solutions to simple problems. These rules address this issue.

85.1 Eliminate clutter.

C provides a rich set of operators and, as a consequence, provides many ways of doing things. It even provides many ways of doing nothing, which is the point of the examples in Table 2

While on the subject of doing nothing, bear in mind that C is happy to permit expressions that do nothing. For example, the following statement, shown in its entirety, is perfectly legal and won't generate even a warning message:

```
a + b;
```

Of course, if you had meant to say

```
a += b;
```

you'd be in trouble.

85.2 Avoid bitwise masks; use bit fields.

A lot of programmers, particularly programmers who started life with assembly language, habitually use bit masks rather than bit fields. I've seen a lot of code like the following:

```
struct fred
{
    int status;
    //...
};

#define CONDITION_A 0x01
#define CONDITION_B 0x02
#define CONDITION_C 0x04

#define SET_CONDITION_A(p)    ((p)->status |=  CONDITION_A)
#define SET_CONDITION_B(p)    ((p)->status |=  CONDITION_B)
#define SET_CONDITION_C(p)    ((p)->status |=  CONDITION_C)

#define CLEAR_CONDITION_A(p) ((p)->status &= ~CONDITION_A)
#define CLEAR_CONDITION_B(p) ((p)->status &= ~CONDITION_B)
#define CLEAR_CONDITION_C(p) ((p)->status &= ~CONDITION_C)

#define IN_CONDITION_A(p)    ((p)->status &   CONDITION_A)
#define IN_CONDITION_B(p)    ((p)->status &   CONDITION_B)
#define IN_CONDITION_C(p)    ((p)->status &   CONDITION_C)

#define POSSIBILITIES(x) ((x) & 0x0030)
#define POSSIBILITY_A    0x0000
#define POSSIBILITY_B    0x0010
#define POSSIBILITY_C    0x0020
#define POSSIBILITY_D    0x0030
```

That's 17 macros to maintain in addition to the field in the data structure, and those macros will

Table 2. How to do nothing in C.

Bad	Good	Comments
`type *end = array;` `end += len-1;`	`type *end` `    =array+(len-1);`	*Initialize in the declaration.*
`while(*p++ != '\0')`	`while( *p++ )`	
`while(gets(buf) != NULL)`	`while( gets() )`	
`if( p != NULL )`	`if( p )`	*!=0 does nothing in a relational expression.*
`if( p == NULL )`	`if( !p )`	
`if(condition != 0)`	`if( condition )`	
`if(condition == 0)`	`if( !condition )`	

`if(condition )`
`    return TRUE;`
`else`
`    return FALSE;`
	`return condition;`	*(or return condition!=0). If it wasn't true, you couldn't get to the* `return TRUE`.

`return condition?0:1;` `return condition?1:0;`	`return !condition;` `return condition!=0;`	*Use the appropriate operator. The relational operators like ! and != all evaluate to 1 or 0 by definition.*

`++x;`
`f(x);`
`--x;`
	`f( x-1 );`	*Don't modify something if you don't need to use the modified value more than once.*

`return ++x;`	`return x+1;`	*See preceding rule.*
`int x;` `f( (int)x );`	`f(x);`	*It's already an int.*
`(void)printf("ok");`	`printf("ok");`	*Just ignore the return value if you're not interested.*

`if      (x > y)`
`else if (x < y)`
`else if (x == y)`
	`if      (x > y)`
	`else if (x < y)`
	`else`
		If it's not > and it's not <, it has to be ==.

`*(p+i)`	`p[i];`	*This one is really an exception to the rule about using pointers presented later in this part. When doing real random access into an array, the bracket notation is easier to read than the pointer version, which is equally inefficient in the random-access case.*

probably be buried in a *.h* file somewhere, not in the file where they are used. The situation would be even worse if you omitted the macros and put the tests directly in the code. Something like:

```
if( struct.status &= ~CONDITION_A )
    //...
```

is difficult to read at best. Even worse is something like this:

```
struct.status = POSSIBILITY_A;
if( POSSIBILITIES(struct.status) == POSSIBILITY_A )
    //...
```

A better solution uses bit fields; they take up no more space and are just as efficient on most machines. (Some people argue that the second example is better than a bit field because there's no implicit shift, but many machines support a bit-test instruction that eliminates any need for a shift, which is a pretty low-overhead operation even if it is used. The need to eliminate unnecessary complexity usually overrides such low-level efficiency considerations.)

```
enum { possibility_a, possibility_b, possibility_c, possibility_d };

struct fred
{
    unsigned in_condition_a : 1;
    unsigned in_condition_b : 1;
    unsigned in_condition_c : 1;

    unsigned possibilities  : 2;
};
```

You now need no macros at all because code like the following is perfectly readable without them:

```
struct fred flintstone;

flintstone.in_condition_a = 1;
if( flintstone.in_condition_a )
    //...

flintstone.possibilities = possibility_b;

if( flintstone.possibilities == possibility_a )
    //...
```

The one obvious exception to this rule is interfacing to memory-mapped hardware; a bit field does not guarantee any sort of ordering in the int from which the bits are carved.

85.3 Don't use "done" flags.

A "done" flag is hardly necessary in C or C++. Using one just adds an unnecessary variable to the subroutine. Don't do this:

```
BOOL done = FALSE;
while( !done )
{
    if( some_condition() )
        done = 1;
}
```

Do this:

```
while( 1 )
{
    if( some_condition() )
        break;
}
```

Many programmers get in the habit of using "done" flags when they learn to program, primarily because languages like Pascal don't support the rich set of control-flow statements available in C.

One exception to this rule is breaking out of nested loops in C++, where a `goto` might cause the code to jump over a constructor or destructor call. This problem was discussed in rule 54.

85.4 Assume that your reader knows C.

Don't do something like this:

```
#define SHIFT_LEFT(x, bits) ((x) << (bits))
```

C programmers know that `<<=` means "shift left." Similarly, don't do things like:

```
x++;     // increment x
```

One problem is that comments like the foregoing often appear in introductory texts on the language because the reader is unfamiliar with C. You shouldn't conclude that just because you see it in such a text that it's a good general practice.

85.5 Don't pretend that C supports a Boolean type (`#define` TRUE).

The following can cause more trouble than not:

```
#define TRUE    1
#define FALSE   0
```

Any nonzero value is "true" in C, so in the following code, `f()` could return a perfectly legitimate "true" value that didn't happen to be 1, and the test will fail:

```
if( f() == TRUE )    // call fails when f returns a true value that isn't 1
    //...
```

The following is safe, but rather awkward; I don't think there's much to recommend the practice:

```
#define FALSE 0
if( f() != FALSE )
    //...
```

The real issue here is really a pretend-C-is-Pascal problem. C, unlike Pascal, doesn't support a native Boolean type, and pretending that it does just gets you into trouble.

Often, the need for an explicit comparison against true or false can be removed by renaming things:

```
if( i_am_sleepy(p) )
```

is much better than:

```
if( sleepy(p) != FALSE )
```

Because it's buried in a macro, a good maintenance programmer cannot make any assumptions about the actual values of TRUE and FALSE. TRUE could be 0 and FALSE be -1, for example. As a consequence, if a function returns an explicit TRUE or FALSE, our diligent maintenance programmer has to spend days making sure that an explicit test for ==TRUE or ==FALSE is used to test the return value of every call (as compared to a simple ! preceding the call, for example). The following:

```
if( i_am_grumpy() )
    ;
```

can no longer suffice because the compiler expects zero for false.

As a final note, bear in mind that the following doesn't work:

```
#define FALSE 0
#define TRUE  !FALSE
```

The !, like all relational operators, evaluates to 1 if the operand is true (nonzero), 0 if not. The foregoing is identical to:

```
#define FALSE 0
#define TRUE  1
```

This is safe but ridiculous:

```
#define IS_TRUE(x)  ((x) != 0)
#define IS_FALSE(x) ((x) == 0)
```

86. 1-bit bit fields should be unsigned.

Ever since ANSI C allowed a bit field to be a signed quantity, I've been seeing code like:

```
struct fred
{
    int i : 1;
}
a_fred;
```

The possible values are 0 and -1. A statement like:

```
#define TRUE 1
//...
if( a_fred.i == TRUE )
    //...
```

doesn't work because a_fred.i can have the value 0 or −1, but it can never be equal to 1. Consequently, the if always fails.

87. Pointers must be above the base address of an array.

This rule was mandated by ANSI C, but many programmers seem unaware of the way the language is supposed to work. ANSI C proclaims that a pointer may go one cell beyond the end of an array, but it may not have a value less than an array's base address. Violating this rule can break code that attempts to run in an 80x86 segmented memory model, for example. The following code won't work:

```
int array[ SIZE ];
int *p = array + SIZE;  // This is okay; you can go one further.
while( --p >= array )    // This doesn't work---possible infinite loop.
    //...
```

The problem is that, in a segmented architecture, it's possible for the array to be at the beginning of a segment—to have an effective address of 0x0000. (In the 8086 architecture, this would be the "offset" component of a segment:offset address.) If p is positioned at the beginning of the array (0x0000), the --p effectively rolls around to 0xfffe (assuming 2-byte ints), which is treated as greater than p. In other words, the previous loop never terminates. Fix the problem like this:

```
while( --p >= array )
{
    //...
    if( p == array )
        break;
}
```

You might be able to get away with a:

```
int *p = array + (SIZE - 1);
do
{
    //...

}while( p-- > array );
```

but be careful that p is in bounds when you enter the loop. (The pointer must be initialized to p+(SIZE-1) rather than p+SIZE.)

88. Use pointers instead of array indexes.

Generally, incrementing a pointer is a better way to go through an array than an array index. For example, a simple loop like the following is tremendously inefficient:

```
struct thing
{
    int field;
    int another_field;
    int another_field;
};

thing array[ nrows ][ ncols ];
int row, col;

for( row = 0; row < nrows ; ++nrows )
    for( col = 0; col < ncols ; ++cols )
        array[row][col].field = 0;
```

The expression:

```
array[row][col]
```

requires two run-time multiplications and an addition. Here's what's really happening:

```
array + (row * size_of_one_row) + (col * size_of_a_thing)
```

Each structure is 12 bytes, and 12 isn't a power of 2, so a more efficient shift can't be used in place of the multiply.

You can do the same thing with a pointer like this:

```
thing *p       = (thing *)array;
int    n_cells = nrows * ncols;
while( --n_cells > = 0 )
    (p++)->field = 0;
```

There are no run time multiplications here at all. The p++ just adds 12 to p.

On the flip side, a pointer is better only when you can increment it—when you're accessing sequential elements. If you're doing true random access into the array, the bracket notation is much easier to read and there's no difference in execution speed.

Similarly, if the innermost part of the loop is inherently inefficient—say for example, we did this:

```
for( row = 0; row < nrows ; ++nrows )
    for( col = 0; col < ncols ; ++cols )
        f( array[row][col]  );
```

and f() took two seconds to execute—then the relative savings of using a pointer are far outweighed by the overhead of the function call, and you can certainly argue that the brackets are more readable. Of course, if f() is a C++ inline function, the function-call overhead might be trivial and a pointer would make more sense, so you could argue that the pointer version is better because overhead is difficult to determine.

Finally, it's true that the optimizer can often transform the array-index version of a loop into a pointerized version, but I think it's bad style to write inefficient code in the hope that the optimizer will clean up after you. Pointers are just as readable as array indexes to someone who knows the language.

89. Avoid goto except...

The rules in this section apply only to C programs. A goto should never be used in C++ for the reasons discussed in rule 54—it's possible for constructors and destructors to not be called.

Generally you should avoid a goto statement, not because a goto is inherently evil, but because there are better ways to do things. C gives you lots of ways to break out of loops other than a goto, for example.

The goto can also hurt readability. I've actually seen code like the following, but it took half an hour to figure out how it worked:

```
while( 1 )
{
    while( condition )
    {
        //...
            while( some_other_condition )
            {
            lab1:
                //...
                goto lab2;
            }
        //...
    }

    if( some_different_condition )
    {
        //...
            if( some_other_condition )
                goto lab1;
            else
            {
            lab2:
        //...
            }
    }
}
```

More the point, after I figured it out, it was easy to rewrite it to eliminate the goto branches.

The readability problem still exists even when an explicit goto isn't there. A switch statement, for example, performs an implicit goto to get to the case statement. The following is legal C, but I wouldn't recommend it:

```
switch( some_condition )
{
case A: if( some_other_condition )
            //...
        else
        {
case b:     //...
        }
}
```

The goto *is* useful in several situations. Here are two:

- Multiple goto branches to a single label preceding a return statement are better than multiple return statements. It's easier to debug such a function because you can set a single breakpoint when you need to trap the exit code. Bear in mind that a goto must precede a statement; it cannot precede a close brace. Use a:

```
        //...
    exit:
        return;
    }
```

if necessary.

- Goto branches in a downward direction that allow an escape from a system of nested loops are better than a "done" flag that has to be tested in every loop-control statement. If each of the while statements in the following code executed 100 times, the done flag would have to be tested 1,000,000 times, even though it's set only on an error condition:

```
int done = 0;
int condition1, condition2, condition3;
//...

while( !done && condition1 )
{
    while( !done && condition2 )
    {
        while( !done && condition3 )
        {
            if( something_terrible )
                done = 1;
        }
    }
}
```

Eliminate the unnecessary million tests with a goto as follows:

```
while( condition1 )
{
    while( condition2 )
    {
        while( condition3 )
        {
            if( something_terrible )
                goto out;
        }
    }
}
out:
    //...
```

The test in a loop-control statement is one place where efficiency is a real consideration because the code is executed many times. This is particularly true in the inner loop-control statements of a nested system. A done flag in an inner test can slow down the execution quite a bit and is best avoided.

Rules for C++ Programming

This part of the book contains rules unique to C++ programming. As I said in the Introduction, this book is not an introduction to C++, so the following rules assume that you at least know the syntax of the language. I don't waste space describing how C++ works. There are lots of good books that teach you C++, including my own *C+C++*. You should also familiarize yourself with object-oriented design principles. I recommend Grady Booch's *Object-Oriented Analysis and Design with Applications*, 2nd ed. (Redwood City: Benjamin Cummings, 1994).

As is the case with the book as a whole, the rules start out addressing general issues, then move on to the specific.

Part 8.A. Design and Implementation Issues.

90. Object-oriented and "structured" designs don't mix.

90.1 If it's not object-oriented, use C.

Let me start by saying that there's absolutely nothing wrong with a well-done structured design. I happen to prefer the OO approach because I seem to think in an OO way, but it would be presumptuous to call OO design "better." I do believe that an OO approach gives you more maintainable code when the program is large. The benefit is less apparent with smaller programs because object-orientation usually adds complexity at the application level. (The main benefit of OO is better maintenance by means of data abstraction, not reduced complexity.)

C++ is particularly intolerant of sloppy design. It's been my experience that C++ programs that don't take a strict object-oriented approach are almost unmaintainable, combining all of the worst features of structured and object-oriented design without reaping any of the benefits of either approach. I don't really buy the argument that you can use C++ as a "better C." The language is too complex—the learning curve too steep—for this to be true. If you don't take advantage of the object-oriented features of the language, there's little point in using it. Using the object-oriented features incorrectly causes even more problems.

Unfortunately, many programmers know how to do object-oriented design but don't actually do it. Excuses range from "It's too much trouble (or I don't have time) to do it right" to "Strict object-oriented design is an academic exercise; there's no time for it in the real world where you have to do things quick and dirty." Perhaps the most disturbing excuse I've heard for bad design (in this case of a class library) was "Not enough of our customers know C++ well enough to use it correctly, so we designed the class library to be easier to use." (Translated into straight talk: Average users are too dumb to do it right; in fact, they aren't even interested in learning how to do it right, and it would be a lot of work to teach them. So, we won't even bother. We'll just dumb down the product.) The problem was compounded by a tutorial that violated object-oriented principles right and left, and unfortunately the tutorial is used by thousands of programmers who don't know any better as an example of how to write an application using this class library. They, quite reasonably, expect the tutorial to show how to do things correctly, so they never suspect that things are deliberately done incorrectly to make the tutorial "easier to understand."

C++ is a difficult language to both learn and use. There are so many details to writing a C++ program that even experienced programmers forget them at times. Moreover, just finding enough C++ programmers to write, much less maintain, your code is a difficult process. You're deluding yourself if you believe that C++ can be used naively. It's too easy for an inexpert programmer to do something wrong and not even know it, making for a very frustrating time tracking down a bug that is recognizable as such. Many of these sorts of bugs even go undetected through initial testing and make it into the final product, making maintenance a shaky proposition.

Why then use C++ at all? The answer is that, *when used properly* C++ gives you significant benefits in maintenance. You can make massive changes in behavior (like translating an entire program from English to Japanese or moving it to a different operating environment) with only a few changes in the source code—all limited to a very small corner of that code. These sorts of changes in a structured system tend to require modification of virtually every function in the program.

If you don't follow the rules, though, you end up with the disadvantages of both systems. Structured designs tend to have problems with coupling relationships not found in a good object-oriented design, but if you go halfway, many of these bugs will be hidden in classes where they will be hard to find. Moreover, object-oriented designs tend to be very complex, and the interrelation between objects is sometimes unpredictable. (That's also one of the main benefits of the methodology; it's possible to model a system so complex that the behavior can't be predicted in advance.) Tools like object diagrams become indispensable because, if the system doesn't work, odds are that it's the message flow that's at fault. If an individual object doesn't work, it's easy to fix provided that the interface is correct because the changes will be limited to a single class definition. When you do things incorrectly, it becomes very difficult to track these problems because back doors are used to pass information, and a change in one class can ripple to other classes.

So, if you "don't have the time to do it right," you're much better off staying with a structured design and a straight C implementation. It will be easier to find bugs because the code will be less compartmentalized and you won't have the added complexity of a message-passing system to distract you. Taking shortcuts now can make a sort-of-object-oriented program unmaintainable a year from now; you might have to throw out the whole program and start over. The promise of better maintenance can only be realized only if you follow the rules.

Because this book isn't an OO-design book, I'll refer you to Booch's book, mentioned in the introduction of this part, if you need to learn about the process of object-oriented design. This book discusses the rules that help that process go more easily.

91. Expect to spend more time in design and less in development.

My experience is that, once you factor out the C++ learning curve, object-oriented (OO) systems take about the same time to develop as structured systems. However, you spend a much higher percentage of the total time in design with an OO approach, and the coding goes faster. In practice, a large project could spend four to six months in design without any code being written. Unfortunately, this is a hard pill for the productivity-equals-lines-of-code-per-day folks to swallow. Because the overall development time is the same, the increase in productivity happens after the code hits maintenance. *Correctly done*, object-oriented systems are easier to code and easier to maintain.

92. C++ class libraries usually can't be used in a naive way.

One of the "big lies" about C++ that's pushed by those salespeople with the pointy teeth and slicked-back hair is that your second-bench C programmers can use class libraries created by the gurus without really needing to know C++. Unfortunately, any but the most trivial class library will use hard-to-understand parts of C++ like inheritance and virtual functions—at least it will if it's designed properly. A library that didn't exploit those features of C++ could just as easily be implemented in C. Users of the library will have to know C++ pretty well by necessity.

Any program written by people who aren't thoroughly versed in whatever language they're using will be at best buggy; at worst, it will be unmaintainable. Probably the hardest bug to find is one that you don't think is a bug. If your understanding of how the language works is imperfect, you might think that there's nothing wrong with a piece of code that is pathologically buggy, because the code looks okay.

The industry has seen this problem before, when COBOL shops were forced to move to C, but the programmers weren't given the training necessary for them to use C correctly. There's a lot of unmaintainable buggy C out there as an object lesson. C++ shows all the signs of being even more of a problem, as managers jump onto the C++ bandwagon without really knowing what they're getting into. A lot of buggy C++ code is being written daily by people that don't know enough of the language to know that they're doing anything wrong.

93. Use checklists.

One of the reasons that C++ has such a steep learning curve is that you have to keep track of so many small details to accomplish even simple tasks. It's easy to forget something, even when you've been doing it for a while. I handle the problem by keeping a few boilerplate template files around—one for each common situation. (I've one for a base-class definition, one for a derived-class definition, and so forth.) I start by copying the appropriate template into my current working file, and then use my editor's search-and-replace feature to fill in the blanks. I'll also move appropriate functions into *.cpp* files when appropriate, and so forth. Listings 5 and 6 show simple template (in the English, not C++ sense) files for base and derived classes (somewhat stripped down from the ones that I actually use, but you get the idea).

Listing 5. *base.tem*— Checklist for a base-class definition.

```
 1    class base
 2    {
 3        cls obj;
 4    public:
 5        virtual
 6        ~base    ( void         );
 7         base    ( void         );
 8         base    ( const base &r );
 9
10        const base &operator=( const base &r );
11    private:
12    };
13    //-------------------------------------------------------------
14    /*virtual*/ ~base::base( void )
15    {
16    }
17    //-------------------------------------------------------------
18    inline base::base( void ) : obj( value )
19    {
20    }
21    //-------------------------------------------------------------
22    inline base::base( const base &r ) : obj( r.obj )
23    {}
24    //-------------------------------------------------------------
25    inline const &base::operator=( const base &r )
26    {
27        if( this != &r )
28        {
29            obj = r.obj;
30        }
31        return *this;
32    }
```

Listing 6. *derived.tem*— Checklist for a derived-class definition.

```
1   class derived : public base
2   {
3       cls obj;
4   public:
5       virtual
6       ~derived      ( void          );
7        derived      ( void          );
8        derived      ( const base &r );
9
10       const derived &operator=( const derived &r );
11
12  private:
13  };
14  //-----------------------------------------------------------------
15  /*virtual*/ ~derived::derived( void )
16  {
17  }
18  //-----------------------------------------------------------------
19  inline derived::derived( void ) : base( value )
20                                  , obj( value )
21  {
22  }
23  //-----------------------------------------------------------------
24  inline derived::derived( const derived &r ) : base ( r       )
25                                              , obj  ( r.obj )
26  {}
27  //-----------------------------------------------------------------
28  inline const &derived::operator=( const derived &r )
29  {
30       if( this != &r )
31       {
32           *((base *)this) = r;
33           obj = r.obj;
34       }
35       return *this;
36  }
```

94. Messages should exercise capabilities, not request information.

Object-oriented and structured systems tend to approach problems in radically different ways. Take the lowly `employee` record as an example. In a structured system, you'd use a `struct` and access fields in that `struct` all over your program. Code to print the record, for example, could easily be duplicated in several hundred places in the code. If you change something basic, like changing the `name` from an array of `char` to an array of 16-bit Unicode characters, you have to ferret out every reference to the `name` and modify it to work with the new type.

In a well-designed object-oriented system, it won't be possible to access the `name` field.[4] Let me repeat that because the concept is so fundamental: It is not possible to access a field inside an object, even something as simple as a name in an `employee` object. Rather you'll ask the `employee` to exercise some capability, such as "print yourself," "flush yourself to the database," or "update yourself by interacting with a user." In the last case, the message handler would throw up the dialog box that the user would use to enter or modify the data.

The main advantage of this approach is that the sender of these messages could care less how the data is stored internally. As long as the object can get itself printed, updated, or whatever, there's no problem. You can change the `name` to Unicode without affecting the sender of the message. Many of the other rules in this part of the book discuss this issue further.

95. You usually cannot convert an existing structured program to object-oriented.

One of the side effects of the organization just described is that it is usually not possible to convert a structured approach to this way of thinking without a complete rewrite of the code. Going back to printing, the message might really be "render yourself onto this device," and the message handler would be passed a reference to a generic `device` object to receive the data. The actual code that does the rendering is effectively *inside* the object. (By way of clarification, there's no reason why several render-yourself messages can't be supported. A spreadsheet object might support render-as-grid, render-as-graph, and render-as-piechart messages, for example.)

In a structured system, the code that does the rendering is *external*. Some function gets an object from somewhere, then make various system calls to get the thing on the screen. If you're talking about `printf()`, the calls aren't very complicated, but if you're talking about Windows or Motif, then you have a problem. The object-oriented design is effectively inside-out with respect to the structured design.

The advantage to the object-oriented approach is that you can change operating environments by changing the `device` implementation, and none of the other code in the program is affected. The changes involved are so fundamental, though, that getting to that point involves rewriting every function in the program that calls an operating-system function directly. This is not a trivial enterprise and will probably involve throwing away the majority of the code in the existing application.

The update-yourself message is similar; the update dialog box would be drawn by external code in a standard structured program. In an OO design, the object itself interacts with the user in response to receiving an update-yourself message—inside out from the structured approach. The advantage, again, is that changes to the fields that have to updated are concentrated in the class definition. You don't have to search the entire program for all the code that uses objects of a class every time a field in the class definition changes.

My experiences with hybrid applications have not been good; They seem to have all the problems of both structured and object-oriented systems without any of the advantages of either. This is the real danger of the "I don't have time to do it right" guys—that they'll end up with an unmaintainable hybrid.

---

4   To be strictly correct, at least in terms of C++ idiom, I should call a "field" a "member data component." It's rather awkward to say "the name member-data component," however, so I'm just going to use "field" when the meaning is clear from context.

It's a mistake to consider a body of existing code, no matter how large, to be an "asset" that you must "leverage." You are not throwing away the money spent to write the existing code if you decide to discard it. The money spent writing the code has probably already paid for itself in sales, and you got to where you are now, not by "leveraging" existing code, but by writing code from scratch. Some start-up company that's nipping at your heals is taking advantage of current technology and current thinking about design methodology by writing their product from scratch. Meanwhile, your existing code is locking you into an obsolete design and out-of-date technology. It's just not possible to sit back and rest on your laurels; you must constantly be rewriting from scratch to improve your product in any but the most incremental way.

I should say that many people disagree with me on this point. A reviewer of a recent article responded to the (perhaps oversimplified) statement that hybrid applications "don't work" by saying "I know tons of shipping applications that are written exactly this way and therefore do work, in that they make a profit for their creators." On the other hand, the fact that this reviewer worked for a company that owned several huge hybrid applications might have colored his comments. One of those hybrids was over a year late at the time that he made his comment, and maintenance was a consistent nightmare on many of the others, but I guess that those issues weren't important enough to consider—this particular programmer didn't do maintenance.

96. A derived class object *is* a base-class object.

97. Derivation is the process of adding member data and methods.

In C++, a derived class can be seen as a mechanism for adding member data and message handlers to an existing class definition—to the base class. (You can also look at derivation as a means of changing the behavior of a base class object when it receives a particular message. I'll look at that use in a moment when I discuss virtual functions.) A class hierarchy, then, is just a means of representing the member data and methods defined for a particular object. An object contains all of the data and methods declared at its level and also at all levels above it.

A common error made by beginning C++ programmers is to look at a class hierarchy and think that messages are passed from derived-class objects to base-class objects. Remember, a class-hierarchy doesn't exist at runtime in C++. All that you have at runtime is the actual objects, whose fields were defined at compile time using the class hierarchy.

The matter is confused by many Smalltalk books that describe the runtime implementation of the message-handling system as if messages are being passed from derived to base-class.[5] This is simply not true (in either Smalltalk or C++). C++ uses inheritance. The derived class *is* the base class, but with a few fields and message handlers added. Consequently, when a C++ object receives a message, it either handles it or it doesn't; either it has defined a handler or it has inherited one. If neither is the case, the message just can't be handled. It isn't passed anywhere.

---

[5] They aren't. Even in Smalltalk, there's only one object, which either receives the message or doesn't. Smalltalk interpreters, however, tend to implement message handling with several tables of function pointers, one for each class. If the interpreter can't find a handler for a message in the derived-class's dispatch table, it searches the base-class table. This mechanism isn't used in C++, which is a compiled language and, therefore, doesn't use multilevel runtime table lookup. Even if all functions in a base class were virtual, for example, the virtual-function table of the derived class would have a slot for each base-class virtual function. The C++ runtime environment doesn't search through a hierarchy of tables, it just uses the table for the current object. More on this in a bit.

Don't confuse the inheritance relationship with *aggregation*. In aggregation, one class *contains* an object of another class (as compared to deriving from another class). Aggregation is actually preferable to derivation when you have a choice because the coupling relations between a contained object and the outside world are much weaker than those between a base class and the outside world.

Aggregation allows the container's methods to act as a filter through which messages destined for the contained object are passed. Often the message handlers will have the same name in the container and the contained object. For example:

```
class string
{
    //...
public:
    const string &operator=( const string &r );
};

class numeric_string     // A string that holds a number
{
    string str;
    //...
public:
    const string &operator=( const string &r );
}

const string &numeric_string::operator=( const string &r )
{
    if( r.all_characters_are_digits() )
        str = r;
    else
        throw invalid_assignment();

    return *this;
}
```

This is actually a rather weak example of aggregation because, if `operator=()` were virtual in the `string` class, `numeric_string` could derive from `string` and override the assignment operator to test for a valid numeric value. On the other hand, if the `string` overloaded + to do concatenation, you might want to overload + in a `numeric_string` to do addition (i.e. convert the strings to numbers, add the numbers, then evaluate to a string that held the result). Aggregation would solve a few problems in this last situation.

Moving back to derivation, objects of the classes shown in Table 3 would probably be layed out identically in memory. Each of these definitions has a `some_cls` component, if you will, but accessing that component requires very different procedures and mechanisms. In this book, I use the phrase "base-class component" to refer to the part of the object that's defined at the base-class level, not to a contained object. Put another way, when I say that a derived-class object has a "base-class component," I mean that some of it's fields and message handlers are defined at the base-class level. When discussing containment, I'll call it a "field" or a "contained object."

Table 3. Two class definitions represented identically in binary

Aggregation	Derivation
| ```
class container
{
    some_cls contained;
    //...
};
``` | ```
class base : public some_cls
{
    //...
};
``` |

98. Design the objects first.

The first order of business should always be designing the messaging system, typically using object diagrams like the ones described by Booch. If you start with the class hierarchy, you tend to over-design, implementing functionality that's not needed. Moreover, without knowing how the objects need to communicate with each other, it's usually difficult to tell in advance what sort of capabilities will be required in each class. It's difficult to generalize when you have no specifics.

99. Design the hierarchy next, from the bottom up.

Once you get the object/messaging system designed, you can start on the hierarchy. Sit back and look at the various objects, and you'll see that many of them receive similar messages. If two messages sent to two different object are close, but not identical, you can usually come up with a slightly more general compromise that can work in both places. The handlers for all common messages should be concentrated into a single base class. For example, given object one, which receives the messages A, B, and C, and object two, which receives A, B, D, and E, you should end up with a small class hierarchy in which a base class implements messages handlers for A and B, one derived class implements a handler for C, and a second derived class implements handlers for D and E. You continue this process of combining common elements into common base classes until there's nothing else to combine. You now have the basic class hierarchy.

You'll note that the more general a class, the higher it is in the hierarchy. For example, a `manager` probably has all the properties of a generic `employee` but a few more properties as well (such as a list of managed employees). It makes sense, then, for `manager` to derive from `employee` because it adds functionality not present in the `employee` base class.

At this stage of the design process, you still haven't even thought about what's going to be in the objects. You're still dealing only with the messaging system.

The last step in this stage of the design—after you've sketched out the complete class hierarchy design—is to write out the class definitions. You'll add a `public` member function for each message that that the object receives. *These message handlers are the only public things in your class definition.* Everything else *must* be `private` or `protected`. More on this shortly.

99.1 Base classes should have more than one derived class.

This is just a different way of looking at the previous rule. If a base class is a way to concentrate like functionality into one place, it makes sense that you'll never have a derived class with no siblings. If you do, the capabilities of this only child should be moved into the parent.

100. The capabilities defined in the base class should be used by *all* derived classes.

101. C++ is not Smalltalk—avoid a common `object` class.

The bottom-up hierarchy-development process typically gives you a forest of small trees, most wider than they are tall. Building a hierarchy from the bottom up helps you avoid a common problem in C++ class hierarchies: a Smalltalk-like `object` class from which everything in the system derives. This is good design in Smalltalk, but usually doesn't work in C++. What functionality could this common `object` implement? That is, what functionality does every object of every class in your program have to have? The only one that I can think of is memory management—the ability for an object to create itself. This is done in C++ using `new`, which is effectively a global-level function. In fact, you can look at the C++ global level as the functional equivalent of the Smalltalk `object`. A good C++ class hierarchy is usually a collection of smaller hierarchies. To quote no less an authority than Bjarne Stroustup—the creator of C++—on the subject:[6]

> *The point here is that styles that are appropriate and well supported in Smalltalk are not necessarily appropriate for C++. In particular, a slavish following of Smalltalk style in C++ leads to inefficient, ugly, and hard to maintain C++ programs. The reason is that good C++ requires design that takes advantage of C++'s static type system rather than fights it. Smalltalk supports a dynamic type system (only) and that view translated into C++ leads to extensive unsafe and ugly casting.*
>
> *... In addition, Smalltalk encourages people to see inheritance as the sole or at least primary way of organizing programs and to organize classes into a single-rooted hierarchies. In C++, classes are types and inheritance is by no means the only means of organizing programs. In particular, templates are the primary means for representing container classes.*

One big problem with a poorly designed hierarchy is excess baggage. Base classes usually have to have fields to support the capabilities exercised by the various handlers. If a derived class doesn't use this capability, then the object is carrying around the overhead without the benefit. That's one of the problems with a Smalltalk-like hierarchy that is rooted in a common object. Any fields that you put there (and any slots in the virtual-function table) will be carried around by every object in the system, whether or not the object uses those fields.

The best way to avoid this problem is to use multiple inheritance to implement *mix-in* classes. Here's how a mix-in works. Returning to our `employee` example, you could implement it as a system of classes as follows:

---

[6]   This quote an excerpt from an essay that Stroustrup posted to BIX in December, 1992. The entire essay is reproduced in Martin Heller's *Advanced Win32 Programming* (New York, Wiley, 1993), pp. 72–78.

```
class employee
{
    // contains all information common to all employees:
    // name, address, etc.
};

class manager : public employee
{
    // adds manager-specific information, such as a list of
    // employees. A manager is also an employee, of course,
    // so derivation is appropriate

    database list_of_managed_employees;
}

class peon : public employee
{
    // add peon-specific information

    manager *the_boss;
}
```

All this is reasonable until it comes time to create our list of `employee` objects for the `manager` to maintain. In many data-structure implementations, an object is made storable by deriving its class from a class that implements those things that the data-structure needs to get its work done. You could do that here with:

```
class storable;

class employee : public storable {/*...*/};
class manager  : public employee {/*...*/};
class peon     : public employee {/*...*/};
```

The `database` class's `add()` method, for example, would take a pointer to a `storable` object as its argument. This way, any `storable` object (or an object of any class that derives from `storable`) can be added to a `database` without needing to modify any of the code that comprises class `database`.

All seems hunky dory until we actually look at the way the classes are used. Let's say that this is an average company where the managers outnumber the peons by a ration of 100 to 1. There are no lists of managers, however, only lists of peons. Nonetheless, every `manager` will carry around the overhead of being `storable`, even though that capability is never used. Solve the problem with multiple inheritance:

```
class storable;

class employee                                  {/*...*/};
class manager  : public employee                {/*...*/};
class peon     : public employee, public storable {/*...*/};
```

The issue here is that "storability" is an attribute of an object. It's not a base class in the standard sense of "a circle *is a* shape," but rather "a peon *is* storable." That missing "a" is important. A base class that implements a "property" like storability is called a *mix-in* class, because you can mix the property into those classes that need it, and only into those classes. One good way to distinguish between these two uses of derivation is that the name of a mix-in class is usually an adjective (storable, sortable, persistent, dynamic, etc.). The name of a true base class is usually a noun.

Because of the nature of C++, there are a few problems with multiple inheritance discussed in all of the textbooks, most caused by a diamond-shaped class hierarchy:

```
class parent {};

class mother : public parent {};
class father : public parent {};

class child : public mother, public father {}
```

There are two difficulties. If `parent` has a method called `go_to_sleep()`, you'd get an error if you tried to send the message like this:

```
child philip;

philip.go_to_sleep();
```

The problem is that there are effectively two `parent` objects in the `child` object. Remember, derivation just adds fields (member data) and message handlers (member functions). A `mother` has a `parent` component: it contains all of the fields of a `parent` in addition to its own.[7] The same goes for the `father`. A `child`, then, has a `mother` and `father`, each of which has a `parent`. The problem with `philip.go_to_sleep()` is that the compiler doesn't know which `parent` should receive the message, the one in the `mother` or the one in the `father`.[8]

One way to solve the problem is with a disambiguating function that directs the message to the correct (or to both) affected classes:

```
class parent { public: go_to_sleep(); };

class mother : public parent {};
class father : public parent {};

class child : public mother, public father
{
public:
    go_to_sleep()
    {
        mother::go_to_sleep();
        father::go_to_sleep();
    }
}
```

Another solution is a `virtual` base class:

---

[7] Don't confuse this process with aggregation. The `mother` does not have a `parent` member, but rather the part of the the `mother` that is defined at the base-class level is characterized as a "parent component."

[8] It's actually more correct, but more confusing, to say that at compile time, the compiler doesn't know from which of the `parent` base classes the `child` inherits the `go_to_sleep()` message handler. You might wonder why the ambiguity matters, because the function is the same in both cases. The runtime ramification is that the compiler doesn't know what value to put into the `this` pointer when it calls the base-class member function.

```
class parent {};

class mother : virtual public parent {};
class father : virtual public parent {};

class child : public mother, public father {}
```

which causes the compiler to put only one `parent` in the `child` that's shared by both `mother` and `father`. The ambiguity goes away, but other problems are introduced. First, there's no way to indicate at the child level whether or not you want the virtual base class. For example, in the following code, the `tree_list_node` can be a member of both a tree and a list at the same time:

```
class node;
class list_node : public node {};
class tree_node : public node {};

class tree_list_node : public list_node, public tree_node {};
```

In the following version, the `tree_list_node` can be a tree member or a list member, but not both at the same time:

```
class node;
class list_node : virtual public node {};
class tree_node : virtual public node {};

class tree_list_node : public list_node, public tree_node {};
```

You'd like to be able to make this decision when you create the `tree_list_node`, but there's no way to do it.

The second problem is initialization. The constructors in the `list_node` and `tree_node` both probably initialize the `node` base class but to different values. If there's only one `node`, which gets to do the initialization? The answer is not pretty. The most derived class (`tree_list_node`) has to initialize the `node`. It's really a bad idea, though, to require a class to know about anything in the hierarchy beyond its immediate parents—otherwise there's too much internal coupling.

The flip side of the same problem shows up when you have `virtual` functions, as in the following code:

```
class persistent
{
public;
    virtual flush() = 0;
};

class doc1: virtual public persistent
{
public:
    virtual flush(){ /* flush doc1 data to disk */ }
};

class doc2: virtual public persistent
{
public:
    virtual flush(){ /* flush doc2 data to disk */ }
};

class superdoc : public doc1, public doc2 {};

persistent *p = new superdoc();
p->flush();                      // ERROR: which flush() function gets called?
```

102. Mix-ins shouldn't derive from anything.

103. Mix-ins should be virtual base classes.

104. Initialize virtual base classes with the default constructor.

You can minimize the problems discussed earlier by trying to adhere to the following rules (many mix-ins can't adhere to all of them, but do your best):

- If possible, a mix-in should not derive from anything, thereby avoiding the diamond-shaped-hierarchy problem entirely.
- It should be possible for a mix-in to be a virtual base class, so that if you do end up with a diamond, the ambiguity problem won't arise.
- If possible, the mix-in should always be constructed using only the default constructor (the one with no arguments). This makes it easier to be a virtual base class because you don't have to worry about initialization by the most-derived object. Default construction is, after all, the default.

105. Derivation is not appropriate if you never send a base-class message to a derived-class object.

106. Choose containment over derivation whenever possible.

107. Use `private` base classes only when you must provide virtual overrides.

The main benefit of derivation is that you can write general code that manipulates generic base-class objects, and this same code can also manipulate derived-class objects (or more precisely, can manipulate the base-class component of the derived-class object). For example, you can write a function that prints a list of shape objects, but the list actually contains objects that derive from shape, such as `circle` and `line`. The print function doesn't need to know this, however. It's quite happy thinking that they're generic shapes. This quality is what people mean when they say `code` reuse. You're reusing the same code to do different things—sometimes it prints a circle, sometimes a line.

If you find yourself with a derived-class object that is never asked to exercise a base-class capability, there's probably something wrong with the hierarchy design, though there are rare situations where this behavior is reasonable; that's why `private` base classes are part of the language. Nonetheless, containment (making the object a field in a class rather than a base class) is always a better choice than derivation (provided, of course, that you have the choice).

If a derived-class object never receives base-class messages, the odds are that the base class component of the derived-class object should actually be a field and that derivation shouldn't be used at all. Rather than this:

```
class derived : private base
{
};
```

you're almost always better off with:

```
class derived
{
    base    base_obj;
};
```

Use `private` base classes only when you must provide derived-class overrides of base-class virtual functions.

One good example of this misuse of derivation is found in many Windows class hierarchies, which derive classes like "dialog box" from "window." In real code, however, you'll never send a window-related message (like "move yourself" or "resize yourself") to a dialog box. That is, a dialog box *is not* a window, at least in terms of how a dialog-box object is used in the program. Rather, a dialog box *uses* a window to display itself. The phrase *is a* implies derivation, while *uses* implies containment—a better choice here.

This bad design, by the way, usually comes about by not following the rule about defining the objects first. That is the concept of a "window" in Microsoft Windows is meaningful only to the display subsystem. A dialog box is represented by a window, bit that doesn't mean that it *is* a window, even if the display subsystem would prefer to look at it that way. The bad design comes from starting out with an existing display system, and then wrapping it with a class library rather than starting with a description of a program, and then deciding how to implement the natural objects in the program.

108. Design the data structures last.

The last thing to do in the design process is to add data fields. In other words, once you get the messages worked out, you need to figure out how to implement the capabilities requested by the messages. This is probably the hardest part of the object-oriented-design process for a structured programmer to do: forcing yourself not to think about the underlying data structure until the entire messaging system and class hierarchy is done.

At this point in the design process, you'll also add `private` "workhorse" (or "helper") functions that help the message handlers get their jobs done.

109. All data in a class definition must be `private`.

110. Never provide public access to `private` data.

All data in a class definition must be `private`. Period. No exceptions. The problem here is the tight coupling between a class and its users when the users access data fields directly. I'll give you a few examples. Let's say that you have a `string` class that uses an array of `char` to store its data. A year from now, you get a client in Pakistan and need to translate all of your strings to Urdu, necessitating a move to Unicode. If your string class allowed any access to a local `char*` buffer, either by making the field public or by defining a function that returned a `char*`, you're in deep trouble.

Let's look at code. Here is a *really* bad design:

```
class string
{
public:
    char *buf;
    //...
};

f()
{
    string s;
    //...
    printf("%s\n", s.buf );
}
```

If you try to change the definition of `buf` to a `wchar_t *` to handle the Unicode (as is mandated by ANSI C), all of the functions that accessed the `buf` field directly are now broken. You'll have to modify every one of them.

Other related problems have to do with internal consistency. If the string object kept an internal `length` field, you could modify the buffer without modifying the length, thereby breaking the string. Similarly, the string's destructor might assume that because the constructor allocated the buffer using `new`, it would be safe to pass the `buf` pointer to `delete`. If you have direct access, however, you could do something like this:

```
string s;
char    array[128];
s.buf = array;
```

and the memory system would blow up when the string went out of scope.

Just making the `buf` field private doesn't help if you still provide access through a function. Listing 7 shows a fragment of a simple string definition that I'll use several times in the remainder of this part. (I've simplified by putting everything in one listing; normally the class definition and the `inline` functions would be in a *.h* file and the rest of the code in a *.cpp* file.)

You'll note that I have deliberately *not* implemented the following function in Listing 7:

```
string::operator const char*(){ return buf; }
```

If I had, I could do the following:

Listing 7. A simple string class.

```
1    class string
2    {
3        char *buf;
4        int  length; // buffer (not string) length;
5
6    public:
7        virtual
8        ~string( void );
9         string( const char *input_str = "" );
10        string( const string &r          );
11
12       virtual const string &operator=( const string &r );
13
14       virtual int operator< ( const string &r ) const;
15       virtual int operator> ( const string &r ) const;
16       virtual int operator==( const string &r ) const;
17
18       virtual void print( ostream &output ) const;
19       //
20   };
21   //-----------------------------------------
22   inline string::string( const char *input_str /*= ""*/ )
23   {
24       length  = strlen(input_str) + 1;
25       buf     = new char[ length ];
26       strcpy( buf, input_str );
27   }
28   //-----------------------------------------
29   inline string::string( const string &r )
30   {
31       length  = r.length;
32       buf     = new char[ length ];
33       strcpy( buf, r.buf );
34   }
35   //-----------------------------------------
36   /*virtual*/ ~string::string( void )
37   {
38       delete buf;
39   }
40   //-----------------------------------------
41   /*virtual*/ const string &string::operator=( const string &r )
42   {
43       if( this != &r )
44       {
45           if( length != r.length )
46           {
47               free( buf );
48               length = r.length;
49               buf     = new char[ length ];
50           }
51           strcpy( buf, r.buf );
52       }
```

don't change string at all!

→

```
Listing 7. continued. . .
 53       return *this;
 54    }
 55
 56    //---------------------------------------
 57    /*virtual*/ int string::operator< (const string &r) const
 58    {
 59       return strcmp(buf,r.buf) <  0;
 60    }
 61    //---------------------------------------
 62    /*virtual*/ int string::operator> (const string &r) const
 63    {
 64       return strcmp(buf,r.buf) >  0;
 65    }
 66    //---------------------------------------
 67    /*virtual*/ int string::operator==(const string &r) const
 68    {
 69       return strcmp(buf,r.buf) == 0;
 70    }
 71    //---------------------------------------
 72    /*virtual*/ void string::print( ostream &output ) const
 73    {
 74       cout << buf ;
 75    }
 76    //---------------------------------------
 77    inline ostream &operator<<( ostream &output, const string &s )
 78    {
 79       // This function is not a member function of class string,
 80       // but does not have to be a friend because I implemented
 81       // a print-yourself method.
 82
 83       s.print(output);
 84       return output
 85    }
```

```
void f( void )
{
    string s;
    //...
    printf("%s\n", (const char*)s );
}
```

but I can't implement an `operator char*()` function that works with a Unicode string, which uses 16-bit bytes. I'd have to provide an `operator wchar_t*` function, then modify the code in `f()` to:

```
printf("%s\n", (const wchar_t*)s );
```

One of the main things that I'm trying to avoid with an object-oriented approach, however, is the need to modify the user of an object when the internal definition of that object changes, so a conversion to char* is unacceptable.

There are problems on the internal-consistency front, too. Given the `buf` pointer returned by `operator const char*()`, you can still modify the string through the pointer and mess up the `length` field, though you'd have to work at it a bit:

```
string s;
//...
char *p = (char *)(const char *)s;
gets( p );
```

An equally serious, but harder to detect, problem appears in the following code:

```
const char *g( void )
{
    string s;
    //...
    return (const char *)s;
}
```

The cast operation calls operator **const char***(), which returns buf. The string class's destructor passes the buffer to delete when the string goes out of scope, however. Consequently, g() returns a pointer to deleted memory. Unlike the earlier example, this second problem doesn't have a convoluted two-part cast to give us a clue that something's wrong.

The implementation in Listing 7 does it right by eliminating the char* conversion in favor of message handlers such as the print-yourself method (print()). I'd print the string with:

```
string s;
s.print( cout )
```

or:

```
cout << s;
```

not by using printf(). There's no public access to the internal buffer at all. The surrounding function could care less how the characters are stored—as long as the string object responds correctly to a print-yourself message. You can change the internals of the string representation as much as you want without affecting the sender of the print() message. For example, the string object could keep two buffers—one for Unicode strings and another for char* strings—and provide translations between them. You could even add a translate_to_French() message and have a multilingual string. This degree of isolation is what object-oriented programming is all about, but you don't get it unless you follow the rules rigidly. There's no room for cowboy programmers here.

110.1 Do not use get/set functions.

This rule is really the same as the previous one "All data must be private." I've separated it out because it's such a common error among beginning C++ programmers. There's no difference between:

```
struct xxx
{
    int x;
};
```

and:

```
class xxx
{
private:
    int x;

public
    void setx( int ix ){ x = ix;    }
    int  getx( void   ){ return x; }
}
```

except that the second version is harder to read. Simply making the data private is not sufficient; you need a change of thinking. To summarize some of the the earlier points:

- A message implements a capability.
- A public function implements a message handler.
- The data fields are irrelevant to the outside world; you add them only to be able to implement a capability. Access should not be possible.

Note that you will occasionally see a message handler that does nothing but return the contents of a field or set a field to a value passed as an argument. This handler is not a get/set function, however. The question to ask is how that situation came about. There's absolutely nothing wrong if you start out with a set of messages, and then decide that the easiest way to implement a message is by putting a dedicated field in the class definition. In other words, this message handler is not a complicated way to access a field; rather, the field is a simple way to implement a message. Though you get to the same place, you got there in a very different way.

Of course, this organization means that C++ can't be used effectively in a hybrid C/C++ environment because the interface between the two halves of the program destroys the encapsulation that you've been trying so hard to implement. In a way, it's a pity that C++ is built on top of C because it just encourages us to do it wrong.

I'll finish this section with a more realistic example. I once saw an interface in which a "calendar" object allowed a user to interactively select a date by clicking on a day displayed on a picture of a calendar. The "calendar" then exported the date to the rest of the program by encapsulating it in a "date" object that was returned from a get_date() message. The problem here is that the design is inside out. The programmer was thinking in a structured, not an object-oriented way.

If properly done, the only object visible to the rest of the program would be the "date" object. The "date" would *use* a "calendar" object to implement an initialize-yourself message (which could be a constructor), but the "calendar" would be contained within the "date." The definition of the "calendar" class might even be nested within the "date" class definition. The "date" object might also support other initialization messages such as initialize-yourself-from-edit-control or initialize-yourself-from-string, but in all cases, it's the responsibility of the "date" object to deal with the user interface needed for initialization. The rest of the program would just use the "date" directly; nobody other than the "date" would even know that a "calendar" object exists. That is, you'd declare a "date" and tell it to initialize itself. You can then pass the "date" object around as needed. Of course, a "date" would also be capable of printing itself, transferring itself to or from a file, comparing itself with other dates, and so forth.

111. Give up on C idioms when coding in C++.

Many of the problems discussed in the previous rules are caused by C programmers unwilling to give up familiar C idioms when they move to C++. The same problem applies to natural languages: You'd have a hard time making yourself understood in French if you just translated English idioms to their literal equivalent.

A good example of this problem in C++ is a `char*`. Most C programmers hate to stop using `char*` for a string. The problem is that you tend to look at a `char*` and think that it *is* a string. It's not. It's a pointer. Pretending that a pointer is a string usually causes problems, some of which I've already discussed and others of which will be discussed later.

Symptoms of this problem are the appearance of `char*` anywhere in a program that supports a `string` class; you should be doing everything in terms of `string`s. To put it more generally: In order to make an object-oriented system work, *everything has* to be an object. The C basic types are not of much use except deep in the bowels of a low-level member function of a low-level class. Encapsulating your `char*` into a `string` class solves lots of problems, and you can waste a lot of time trying to support `char*` when a perfectly good `string` exists and can do the job.

A class definition does not need to add much overhead, so that's not an excuse. If your `string` class has a single `char*` field and if all the methods are `inline` functions, you have no more overhead than you would had you used the `char*` directly, but you'll have all the maintenance benefits available to a C++ class. Moreover you'll be able to do things like derive a class from `string`; you can't derive from `char*`.

Take a Windows edit control—a small window into which the user types data—as an example. (For you X-Window programmers, a Windows "control" is the rough equivalent of a "widget.") An edit control has all of the properties of both a window and a string, and as a consequence, you'd like to implement one by deriving simultaneously from a `window` class and a `string` class.

112. Design with derivation in mind.

Never assume that a class will never be used as a base class. A case in point was the edit-control example mentioned in the previous rule. I'd like to implement one by deriving simultaneously from a `window` class and a `string` class, because an edit control has the properties of both. I won't be able to pull it off unless many of the `string` functions are virtual. That is, because I can do the following with a string:

```
string str = "xxx"; // initialize string to hold "xxx"
str = "Abc";        // Replace previous contents with "abc"
str += "def";       // concatenate "def" to the string.
```

I'd like to be able to do the following to put text in both the buffer maintained by the edit control and the corresponding window as well:

```
class edit_control : public string
                   , public window
{/*...*/};

edit_control  edit = "xxx";
edit =  "Abc";
edit += "def";
```

I'd also like to pass my `edit_control` object to a function that expected a `string` argument, and any changes that function made to (what it thought was) the `string` would automatically appear in the edit-control window, too.

None of this is possible if functions like `operator=()` and `operator+=()` aren't `virtual` in the `string` class, thereby allowing me to change their behavior in the `edit_control` derived class. For example, because the `operator=()` function of the `string` class in Listing 7 on page 111 is virtual, I can do the following:

```
class edit_control : public string
                   , public window
{
    //...
    virtual string &operator=( const string &r );
}

virtual string &edit_control::operator=( const string &r )
{
    *(string *)this   = r;
    window::caption() = r;   // The window:: is just for clarity.
}
```

The following function could be passed either a simple `string` object or an `edit_control` object; it doesn't know or care which it is:

```
f( string *s )
{
    //...
    *s = "New value" ;
}
```

In the case of a `string` object, the internal buffer is updated. In the case of an `edit_control`, the buffer is updated, but the caption of the window is modified, too.

112.1 A member function should usually use the `private` data of a class.

Because all `public` member functions are message handlers and all `private` functions and data just support the `public` message handlers, there's something wrong if a function doesn't either access member data or call a function that accesses member data. That function should probably be moved out to the global level or moved into a different class.

One clear indication that you've done something wrong is a function in one class that requires access to fields from an object of another class to do its work (as compared to having a pointer to another object to be able to send that object messages). In a worst-case scenario, class "host" grants `friend` status to class "guest," and a member function of class "guest" uses a "host" pointer to access the fields of class "host" but doesn't access any fields of its own class at all. The `friend` mechanism is often misused in this way, but a class should grant friendship only so that the friend can send private messages to the granting class. A `friend` class should never access the data members of another class; the coupling is too strong.

You see this error a lot in document/view architectures like MacApp and MFC. Architecturally, a "document" contains the data, and a "view" implements a user interface. The difficulty arises when you want to display some data in your "view." Never allow the "view" to access fields of the "document" to display those fields. The data of any class—including a "document"—should be a carefully guarded secret. A better approach has the "view" passing the "document" a "render your-self into this window" message.[9]

113. Use const.

The const storage class is often omitted from C programs. This is really just sloppiness, but it has little effect on functionality in C. Because C++ is much pickier about types than C, this is a much bigger issue in C++. You should use const whenever possible; it makes the code more robust, and sometimes the compiler will not accept code that doesn't use it. It's particularly important to:

- Always pass pointers to const objects if you're not modifying the object. The declaration:

```
puts( const char *p )
```

tells the compiler that puts() is not going to modify the chars in the array passed via p. That's an extremely useful piece of information for maintenance.
- All messages that do not change the internal state of an object should be declared with const, like this:

```
class cls
{
public:
    int operator==( const cls &p ) const;
};
```

(It's the const on the far right I'm talking about here.) This const tells the compiler that it's safe to pass the message to an object that's declared const. Note that this const at the far right effectively creates the following definition for this:

```
const current_class *this;
```

If code in this const function tried to modify any of the class's data fields or if a call to another member function that was not marked const were attempted, you'd get an error message on the order of "cannot convert pointer to const current_class to pointer to current_class." The pointer in question is this, and it's never legal to implicitly convert a pointer to a constant into a pointer to a variable (because you could then modify the constant through the pointer).

const references are also important and are discussed later.

114. Use struct only if everything's public and there are no member functions.

This rule is a variant on the "If it looks like C, then it acts like C" principle. Use struct only when you're doing C-like things.

Another thing to avoid is derivation from a struct. If I've gotten nothing else across, I hope I've made the point about nothing-but-private data clear. Given the problems of direct access to public data, you can understand why the following is not a great idea:

---

9   Users of MFC can refer to my article "Rewriting the MFC Scribble Program Using an Object-Oriented Design Approach," *Microsoft Systems Journal* 10:8 (August, 1995) for a more in-depth discussion of this topic.

```
typedef struct tagSIZE  // Existing definition from a C .h file
{
    LONG        cx;
    LONG        cy;
}
SIZE;

class CSize : public SIZE   // Definition in a C++ file
{
    //...
}
```

I've seen class definitions like the foregoing that require you to access the cx and cy fields of the base class through a derived-class pointer in order to get at the height. For example:

```
CSize some_size;
some_size.cy;         // ugh!
```

You ought to be able to say:

```
some_size.height();
```

The foregoing code has another, subtler problem. Derivation from an existing C structure is often done by programmers who hope to be able to pass a C++ object to an existing C function. That is, the programmer is assuming that because derivation *effectively* adds fields to a base class, a derived class will *literally* be layed out exactly like the base class, but with a few extra fields tacked on. This might not be true, however. If the derived class adds a virtual function, for example, the base class might have a virtual-function-table pointer added *above* it. Similarly, if the derived class uses multiple inheritance to derive simultaneously from a C struct and something else, there's no guarantee that the C struct will be at the top.

115. Don't put function bodies into class definitions.

There are several problems here. When you actually put the function body in a class definition, like this:

```
class amanda
{
public:
    void peekaboo( void ){ cout << "peek a boo\n"; }
}
```

C++ makes the class inline. The first problem is that these functions tend to grow over time to be too large to be an inline function. It's best to put your inline function definitions outside the class definition but still in the same *.h* file as the class definition:

```
class amanda
{
public:
    void peekaboo( void );
}

void amanda::peekaboo( void )
{
    cout << "peek a boo\n";
}
```

Even more of a problem than size is clutter. Often, the class definition is the only hard documentation you have of the class members. You really want the whole thing to fit on one page, and you want the definition to provide a concise list of function prototypes. If the function and argument names are chosen carefully, this is often all of the documentation you'll need.

As soon as you start adding function bodies—even bodies as short as one line—to the class definition, you lose this clarity. The class definition starts going out to several pages, and it becomes hard to find things, ruining the class definition as a documentation tool.

The third problem is more insidious and can waste hours if you're not careful. Consider the fragment of a linked-list implementation in Listing 8 (which will not compile). The linked_list and the list_node classes send messages to each other. The compiler must see a class definition before it can permit you to send a message to an object of that class. (You can declare a pointer to an object just by seeing a class xxx;, but you can't do anything with that pointer until the entire class definition is processed.) Because inline functions are used in Listing 8, there's no way you can arrange the class definitions to avoid forward references. You can solve the problem by putting the function definitions down at the bottom of the file where they belong. I've done that in Listing 9.

Listing 8. A fragment of a linked-list implementation

```
1    class list_node;
2
3    class linked_list
4    {
5        int        number_of_elements_in_list;
6        list_node *root;
7
8    private:                          // this section contains messages
9        friend class list_node;      // received only from list_node objects
10       void have_removed_an_element(void)
11       {
12           --number_of_elements_in_list;
13       }
14
15   public
16       void remove_this_node( list_node *p )
17       {
18           // The following line generates a compiler error because
19           // the compiler doesn't know that a list_node has a
20           // remove_yourself_from_me( &root ) message.
21
22           p->remove_yourself_from_me( &root );
23       }
24
25       //...
26   };
27
28   class list_node
29   {
30       linked_list *owner;
31   private:                          // This section contains messages
32       friend class linked_list:     // received only from linked_list objects
33
34       void remove_yourself_from_me( list_node *root )
35       {
36           //... Do the removal
37           owner->have_removed_an_element();
38       }
39   };
```

Listing 9. An improved fragment of a linked-list implementation

```
 1   class list_node;
 2
 3   class linked_list
 4   {
 5       int       number_of_elements_in_list;
 6       list_node *root;
 7
 8   private:
 9       friend class list_node;
10       void have_removed_an_element( void );
11
12   public
13       void remove_this_node( list_node *p );
14
15       //...
16   };
17   //====================================================================
18   class list_node
19   {
20       linked_list *owner;
21   private:                          // this section contains messages
22       friend class linked_list:     // received only from linked_list
23                                     // objects
24
25       void remove_yourself from_me( list_node *root );
26   };
27
28   //====================================================================
29   // linked_list functions:
30   //====================================================================
31   inline void linked_list::remove_this_node( list_node *p )
32   {
33       p->remove_yourself_from_me( &root );
34   }
35   //--------------------------------------------------------------------
36   inline void linked_list::have_removed_an_element(void)
37   {
38       --number_of_elements_in_list;
39   }
40
41   //====================================================================
42   // list_node functions:
43   //====================================================================
44   void list_node::remove_yourself_from_me( list_node *root )
45   {
46       //... Do the removal
47       owner->have_removed_an_element();
48   }
```

116. Avoid function overloads and default arguments.

This rule does not apply to constructors and operator-overload functions.

Function overloading, like many other features of C++, was added to the language for specific reasons. Don't get carried away with it. Functions that do different things should have different names.

Function overloads usually cause more problems than they solve. First, there's the ambiguity problem:

```
f( int, long );
f( long, int );

f( 10, 10 );    // ERROR: Which f() do I call?
```

More insidious is:

```
f( int    )
f( void* );

f( 0 );      // ERROR: Call is ambiguous.
```

The problem here is C++, which says that 0 can be treated as a pointer as well as an int. If you do this:

```
const void *NULL = 0;
const int   ZERO  = 0;
```

you can say f(NULL) to pick the pointer version and f(ZERO) to get the int version, but that's an awful lot of clutter. You're better off just using two function names.

Default arguments, which effectively create function overloads (one for each possible combination of arguments) also cause problems. For example, if you say:

```
f( int x = 0 );
```

then *accidentally* call f() without an argument, the compiler will happily and silently provide a zero. All you've done is eliminated what would otherwise have been a useful compile-time error message and moved the error into runtime.

Exceptions to the foregoing include operator overloads and constructors; most classes have several, and default arguments often make sense with constructors. Code like the following is perfectly reasonable:

```
class string
{
public:
    string( char *s = ""     );
    string( const string &r  );
    string( const CString &r ); // conversion from MFC class.
    //...
};
```

As a point of clarification, different classes will often handle the same message by implementing identically named message-handler functions. For example, most classes implement a print() message. The point that I'm trying to make here is that it's a bad idea for a single class to have multiple message handlers with the same name. Rather than:

```
class string
{
    //...
public:
    print( FILE     *fp  );
    print( iostream &ios );
    print( window   &win );
```

I'd recommend:

```
class string
{
    //...
public:
    print_file   ( FILE     *fp  );
    print_stream ( iostream &ios );
    print_window ( window   &win );
```

Even better, if you had a device class that could represent a FILE, an iostream, or a window, depending on how it was initialized, you could implement a single print() function that took a device argument.

I must say that I occasionally violate this rule myself, but I do it knowing that I might be causing trouble for myself down the line.

Part 8.B. Coupling Issues

The concept of coupling was described earlier in a general sense. I've also covered the most important C++ rule for reducing coupling relations: "All data must be private." The idea of minimizing coupling is really central to C++. You can argue that the main purpose of object-oriented design is to minimize coupling relationships by means of encapsulation. This section contains C++ -specific rules that affect coupling.

117. Avoid `friend` classes.

Coupling comes in degrees. A tight coupling between classes happens when you use the `friend` keyword. In this case, when you change anything in a class that grants `friend` status, you also have to examine every function in the `friend` class as well to make sure it still works.

This characteristic is obviously undesirable; you really want to limit the access provided by the `friend` mechanism. I'd like something that worked like `protected` but applied to `friend`s. In a linked list, for example, I'd like to allow a `list_node` object to send a handful of messages to a `list` object, but I don't want these messages to be implemented with `public` functions because nobody except `list_node` objects will send them. My `list` can make these functions `private` and grant `friend` status to the `list_node`, but the `list_node` can then access every private member of a `list`. What I really want is: "Member functions of this `friend` class can call these three private member functions but can't access anything else that's private." Unfortunately, C++ provides no way to limit access to a limited set of message handlers; it's all or nothing.

Though we're stuck with this behavior, we can at least limit the damage by agreement. In other words, we can grant `friend` status with the tacit understanding that the `friend` won't access anything except a limited number of functions in the granting class. Document this relationship as follows:

```
class granting
{
    //...

private: friend class grantee

    // Functions defined in this section will be accessed by
    // members of class grantee but are not available for
    // public use.

    message_sent_from_grantee();
    another_message_sent_from_grantee();

private:

    // True private functions go here. Though the grantee
    // could access these functions, it won't.

    //...
};
```

Remember, we're not really limiting the friendship; this is just a notational convention to help the reader of our class definition divine our intent. Hopefully, whoever is writing the `grantee` class will be grown up enough to not impose on our friendship with unwelcome advances.

118. Inheritance is a form of coupling.

Inheritance is not a panacea because it is, after all, a form of coupling. When you change the base class, the change affects all derived-class objects and all users of derived-class objects (who might be passing it messages, handlers for which are inherited from the base class). In general, you should make your class hierarchies as shallow as possible to minimize this rippling effect. By the same token, the `protected` storage class is suspect because there is a tighter coupling between base and derived class than there would be if the derived class used only the public interface to the base class.

119. Don't corrupt the global name space: C++ issues.

The class definition provides a great way to get symbols out of the global name space because these symbols must either be accessed through an object or with an explicit class name. `x.f()` is a different function than `y.f()` when x and y are objects of different classes. Similarly `x::f()` is a different function from `y::f()`. You should look at the class name and `::` as effectively part of the function name that can be omitted only when something else (like a `.` or `->`) serves as a disambiguator.

I often use an `enum` to limit a constant symbol to class scope:

```
class tree
{
    enum { max_nodes = 128 };

public:
    enum traversal_mechanism { inorder, preorder, postorder };

    print( traversal_mechanism how = inorder );
    //...
}

//...
f()
{
    tree t;
    //...
    t.print( tree::postorder );
}
```

The `tree::postorder` constant passed to `print()` is effectively not in the global name space because the `tree::` prefix is required to access it. There is no name conflict if another class has a member named `postorder` because that member would be named `other_class::postorder` if used externally. Furthermore, the constant `max_nodes` is `private`, so it can be accessed only by member functions and friends of `class tree`—an even further limitation of scope.

One advantage of an `enum` over a `const` member of the class is that the value can be initialized right in the class declaration. A `const` member would have to be initialized in the constructor function, which could be in a different file. An `enum` can also be used as the size in an array declaration and as a `case` in a `switch`; a `const` won't work in either place.

A const member does have its uses. First, you can put non-int-sized things into it. Second, you can initialize it at runtime. Consider the following C++ global-variable definition:

```
const int default_size = get_default_size_from_ini_file();
```

The value is read from the file as the program boots, and this value can't be changed while the program is running.

The foregoing also applies to const class members, which can be initialized from a constructor argument but can't be changed by the member functions. Because a const object cannot appear to the left of an equal sign, const members must be initialized using the member-initialization list as follows:

```
class fixed_size_window
{
    const size height;
    const size width;

    fixed_size_window( size the_height, size the_width )
                                , height( the_height )
                                , width ( the_width  )
    {}
}
```

Nested classes are also useful. You'll often need to create an "auxiliary" class that your user doesn't even know about. For example, the code in Listing 10 implements class int_array, a dynamic two-dimensional array whose size doesn't need to be known until runtime. You can access elements using standard C/C++ array syntax (a[row][col]). An int_array does this using an auxiliary class about which the user of the int_array knows nothing. I've used a nested definition to remove this auxiliary-class definition from the global name space. Here's how it works: The expression a[row][col] evaluates as (a[row])[col]. The a[row] calls int_array::operator[](), which returns an int_array::row object that references an entire row. The [col] is applied to that int_array::row object, causing int_array::row::operator[]() to be called. This second version of operator[]() returns a reference to an individual cell. Note that the constructor of class int_array::row is private because I don't want Joe User to be able to manufacture one. The row must grant friend status to the int_array so that the int_array can create a row.

Listing 10. Auxiliary classes.

```
 1   #include <iostream.h>
 2
 3   class int_array
 4   {
 5       class row
 6       {
 7           friend class int_array;
 8           int *first_cell_in_row;
 9
10           row( int *p ) : first_cell_in_row(p) {}
11       public:
12           int &operator[]( int index );
13       };
14
```

➡

Listing 10. continued...

```
15        int nrows;
16        int ncols;
17        int *the_array;
18
19    public:
20        virtual
21        ~int_array( void          );
22         int_array( int rows, int cols  );
23
24        row operator[](int index);
25    };
26    //=====================================================================
27    // int_array members
28    //=====================================================================
29    int_array::int_array( int rows, int cols )
30                    : nrows      ( rows )
31                    , ncols      ( cols )
32                    , the_array ( new int[rows * cols] )
33    {}
34    //--------------------------------------------------------------------
35    int_array::~int_array( void )
36    {
37        delete [] the_array;
38    }
39    //--------------------------------------------------------------------
40    inline int_array::row int_array::operator[](int index )
41    {
42        return row( the_array + (ncols * index) );
43    }
44    //=====================================================================
45    // int_array::row members
46    //=====================================================================
47    inline int &int_array::row::operator[]( int index )
48    {
49        return first_cell_in_row[index];
50    }
51
52    //=====================================================================
53    void main( void )
54    {
55        int_array    ar(10,20);  // same as ar[10][20], but sizes don't
56                                 // need to be known at compile time.
57        ar[1][2] = 100;
58        cout << ar[1][2];
59    }
```

Part 8.C. References

120. Reference arguments should always be const.
121. Never use references as outputs, use pointers.

Reference arguments are in the language for four reasons:

- You need them to define a copy constructor.
- You need them to define operator overloads. If you defined:

```
some_class *operator+( some_class *left, some_class *right );
```

  you'd have to do addition like this:

```
some_class x, y;
x = *(&x + &y)
```

  Using references for the argument and return value lets you say:

```
x = x + 1;
```

- You often want pass objects by value for semantic reasons. For example, you typically pass a double to a function, not a pointer to a double. Nonetheless, a double is really an 8-byte packed structure with three fields in it: a sign bit, a mantissa, and an exponent. Pass a reference to a const object in this situation.
- When an object of some user-defined class would normally be passed by value, use a reference to a const object instead to avoid the implicit copy-constructor call.

References are not in the language to mimic Pascal, and they should not be used the way that a Pascal program uses them.

The problem with reference arguments is maintenance. Last year, one of your coworkers wrote the following subroutine:

```
void copy_word(char *target, char *&src) // src is a reference to a char*
{
    while( isspace(*src) )
        ++src;                      // Increment the pointer
                                    // referenced by src.
    while( *src && !isspace(*src) )
        *target++ = *src++;         // Advance the pointer
                                    // referenced by source to
}                                   // just past the current word.
```

The author intended you to call copy_word() multiple times. Each time, the subroutine would copy the next word to the target buffer and advance the source pointer.

Yesterday, you wrote the following code:

```
f( const char *p )
{
    char *p = new char[1024];
    load( p );

    char word[64];
    copy_word( word, p );
    delete( p );              // Surprise! p has been modified so the memory
}                             // pool has just blown up!
```

The main problem is that, looking at the copy_word(word,p) call, you haven't a clue that p will be changed by the subroutine. You'd have to go look up the function prototype (which is probably nested six levels deep in #include files) to get this information. The maintenance problems are immense.

If something looks like a normal C function call, it should act like a normal C function call. If the author of copy_word() had used a pointer for the second argument, the call would have looked like this:

```
copy_word( word, &p );
```

That extra & is critical. The average maintenance programmer will assume that the only reason to pass the address of a local variable to another function is to permit that function to modify the local variable. In other words, the pointer version is self-documenting; you're telling your reader that the object is changed by the function. A reference argument doesn't give you this information.

This is not to say that you should avoid references. The fourth reason at the beginning of this section is perfectly legitimate; references are great ways to avoid the copy overhead implicit in a pass by value. To make things safe, though, reference arguments should always reference const objects. Given this prototype:

```
f( const some_class &obj );
```

this code is perfectly legal:

```
some_class an_object;
f( an_object );
```

It looks like a call by value, and more importantly, it acts like a call by value—the const prevents f() from modifying an_object. You get the efficiency of a call by reference without the problems.

To summarize: I decide whether or not to use a reference, first by ignoring the fact that references exist. Function inputs are passed by value and output arguments use pointers to the place in which the output value will be stored. I then convert those arguments that are passed by value into references to const objects if they are:

- objects of some class (as compared to basic types like int)
- not modified anywhere in the function

Objects that are passed by value and then modified inside the function must still be passed by value, of course.

To round things out, here's a real-world example of how *not* to use references. The CDocument object maintains a list of CView objects. You can access the members of this list as follows:

```
CDocument *doc;
CView     *view;

POSITION pos = doc->GetFirstViewPosition();
while( view = GetNextView(pos) )
    view->Invalidate();
```

There are two problems. First, `GetNextView()` is a lousy name. It should be called `GetCurrentViewAndAdvancePosition()` because it really returns the current thing, and then advances the position pointer (which is a reference-argument output) to the next thing. Which brings us to the second point: The average reader is going to look at the previous code and wonder how the loop terminates. In other words, there's a surprise here. The advance operation is obfuscated by hiding it in `GetNextView(pos)`, so it becomes unclear where the advance happens. Matters would be made worse if the loop were larger and contained several functions that took `pos` as an argument; you'd have no idea which function advanced the position.

There are lots of better ways to solve this problem. The simplest is to use a pointer argument to `GetNextView()` rather than a reference:

```
POSITION pos = doc->GetFirstViewPosition()
while( p = GetNextView( &pos ) )
    view->Invalidate();
```

This way, the `&pos` tells you that `pos` will be modified; why else pass a pointer? There are lots of better solutions, however. Here's one:

```
for( CView *p = doc->GetFirstView(); p ; p = p->NextView() )
    p->Invalidate();
```

Here's another:

```
POSITION pos = doc->GetFirstViewPosition();
for(; pos ; pos = doc->GetNextViewPosition(pos) )
    (pos->current())->Invalidate();
```

Here's a third:

```
CPosition pos = doc->GetFirstViewPosition();
for(; pos ; pos.Advance() )
    ( pos->CurrentView() )->Invalidate();
```

Here's a fourth:

```
ViewListIterator cur_view = doc->View_list();   // Iterate across the
                                                // document's list of
                                                // Views.
for(; cur_view ; ++cur_view )          // ++ advances to the next View.
    cur_view->Invalidate();            // -> returns a View*.
```

There are probably a dozen more possibilities. All of the foregoing have the desirable characteristic that there are no hidden operations. It's clear how the "current position" is advanced.

122. Do not return references (or pointers) to local variables.

This problem also appears in C, where you can't return a pointer to a local variable. Don't return a reference to an object that won't exist after the return. The following code doesn't work:

```
some_class &f()
{
    some_class x;
    //...
    return x;
}
```

The real problem here is the syntax of C++. The `return` statement can be some distance from the definition of the return value. The only way to know what `return x` is actually doing is to look at the top of the function and see whether or not it returns a reference.

123. Do not return references to memory that came from `new`.

Every call to `new` must be matched with a `delete`—just like `malloc()` and `free()`. I've sometimes seen people trying to get around the copy-constructor overhead of a binary-operator overload like this:

```
const some_class &some_class::operator+( const some_class &r ) const
{
    some_class *p - new some_class;
    //...
    return *p;
}
```

This code doesn't work because you can't get the memory back to delete it. When you say

```
some_class a, b, c;

c = a + b;
```

The `a+b` returns an object, not a pointer. The only way to get a pointer that you can pass to `delete` is with:

```
some_class *p;
c = *(p = &(a + b));
```

That's too ugly for words.

The `operator+()` function can't return a pointer directly. If it looked like this:

```
const some_class *some_class::operator+( const some_class &r ) const
{
    some_class *p = new some_class;
    //...
    return p;
}
```

You'd have to say:

```
c = *(p = a + b);
```

which is not as ugly as the earlier example, but it's still pretty bad. The only solution to this problem is to grit your teeth and return an object:

```
const some_class some_class::operator+( const some_class &r ) const
{
    some_class obj;
    //...
    return obj;
}
```

If you get a copy constructor call in the return statement, so be it.

Part 8.D. Constructors, Destructors, and `operator=()`

`Constructors, destructors, and operator=()` functions are special in that the compiler generates them if you don't. The compiler-generated default constructor (the one with no arguments) and the compiler-generated destructor are needed to set up the virtual-function table pointer (more on this shortly).

The compiler-generated copy constructor (the one whose argument is a reference to the current class) is needed for two reasons in addition to the virtual-function table. First, C++ code that looks like C must act like C. Because the rules about copying that apply to a `class` also apply to a `struct`, the compiler will typically have to generate a copy constructor in a `struct` to handle C-style structure copying. The copy constructor is used explicitly like this:

```
some_class x;       // default constructor
some_class y = x;   // copy constructor
```

but it's also used implicitly in two situations. The first is a call by value:

```
some_class x;
f( some_class x );  // passed by value, not by reference.

//...                // copy constructor is called to pass x by value. It has
f( x );             // to be copied onto the stack.
```

The second is a return by value:

```
g()                 // Remember that x is a local, automatic variable. It
{                   // goes away when the function returns. The return
    some_class x;   // statement, then must copy x somewhere safe
    return x;       // (typically onto the stack, below the arguments).
}                   // It uses the copy constructor for this purpose.
```

The compiler-generated `operator=()` function is needed only to support C-style structure copying where no assignment operation is defined.

124. `Operator=()` should return a `const` reference.

125. Assignment to self must work.

The `operator=()` definition should always take the following form:

```
class class_name
{
    const class_name &operator=( const class_name &r );
};

const class_name &class_name::operator=( const class_name &r )
{
    if( this != &r )
    {
        // do the copying here
    }
    return *this;
}
```

The argument, which represents the source operand, is a reference to avoid the overhead of a call by value; it's a reference to a const because it's not going to be modified.

The function returns a reference because it can. That is, you could remove the & from the return-value declaration, and everything would work fine, but you'd have an unnecessary call to the copy constructor, necessitated by the return by value. Because we already have an object that's initialized to the right value (*this), we can just return that. Even though it's really a bug for operator=() to return an object rather than a reference, the compiler will just do what you tell it. There will be no error message; and in fact, everything will work. The code will just run more slowly than necessary.

Finally, operator=() must return a const reference simply because you don't want anyone to be able to modify the returned object after the assignment occurs. The following will be illegal if a const reference is returned:

```
(x = y) = z;
```

The reason is that (x=y) evaluates to operator=()'s return value: a const reference. The receiver of the =z message is the object just returned from the x=y. You can't send an operator=() message to a const object, however, because the declaration doesn't have a trailing const:

```
                              // DON'T DO THIS
                              // IN AN operator=()
                              // FUNCTION.
                              //        |
                              //        V
const class_name &operator=( const class_name &r ) const;
```

The compiler should give you an error on the order of "cannot convert reference to variable to reference to const" if you try (x=y)=z.

The other issue in the earlier code is the test:

```
if( this != &r )
```

in the operator=() function. The expression:

```
class_name x;
//...
x = x;
```

must always work, and a test of this against the address of the incoming right argument is the easiest way to make sure. Bear in mind that many algorithms assume that an assignment to self is harmless, so don't make it a special case. Also bear in mind that assignment to self might be obscured by a pointer, as in:

```
class_name array[10];
class_name *p = array;
//...
*p = array[0];
```

126. Classes having pointer members should always define a copy constructor and operator=().

When a class doesn't supply copy heuristics—a copy constructor and `operator=()` function—the compiler does. The compiler-supplied constructor is supposed to do a "member-wise" copy that is supposed to work as if you had said `this->field = src.field` for every member. This means that, in theory, the copy constructors and `operator=()` functions of the contained objects and base classes should be called. Even when everything works right, though, pointers are copied as pointers. That is, a "string" represented by a `char*` is not a "string," it's a pointer, and only the pointer will be copied. Imagine that the `string` definition back in Listing 7 on page 111 didn't have a copy constructor or `operator=()` function. If you say:

```
string s1   "foo", n?;
//...
s2 = s1;
```

the assignment would overwrite the pointer member of `s2` with the pointer from `s1`. Whatever memory that was addressed by `s1->buf` is now lost, so you have a memory leak. Worse, if you change `s1`, `s2` changes too because they're both pointing at the same buffer. Finally, when the strings go out of scope, both strings will pass `buf` to delete, effectively deleting the same memory twice and probably corrupting the memory pool. Solve the problem by adding a copy constructor and `operator=()`, as was done in Listing 7 on page 111. Now the copy will have its own buffer which has the same contents as the source string's buffer.

One last note: I said "supposed to" and "in theory" in the first paragraph because I've seen compilers that effectively did a `memcpy()` as the default copy operation, just as a C compiler would do. In this case, the contained object's copy constructor and `operator=()` will not be called. and you'll *always* have to provide a copy constructor and `operator=()` function to copy contained objects. If you want to play it absolutely safe, you'll do this for all classes that contain members that are anything except basic C numeric types.

127. If you can access an object, it has been initialized.

128. Use member-initialization lists.

129. Assume that members and base classes are initialized in random order.

A lot of inexperienced C++ programmers avoid member-initialization lists, I suppose, because they look so weird. The fact is that most code that does not use them is simply incorrect. Take the following code, for example (assume the string-class definition from Listing 7 on page 111):

```
class base
{
    string s;
public:
    base( const char *init_value );
}
//-----------------------------------
base::base( const char *init_value )
{
    s = init_value;
}
```

The basic principle is: if you can access an object, it has been initialized. Because the s field is visible to the base constructor, C++ guarantees that it is initialized before the body of the constructor is executed. The member initialization list is the mechanism for choosing which constructor to execute. If you leave it out, as is the case in the previous code, you'll get the default constructor—the one with no arguments or, in the case of the string class that we're looking at, the one whose arguments all default to some value. Consequently, the compiler will first initialize s to an empty string, allocating a one-character string from new and initializing it to hold a \0. Then the body of the constructor is executed, and string::operator=() is called. This function deletes the buffer that we just allocated, allocates a longer buffer, and initializes it to init_value. That's an awful lot of work. It's better just to get the thing initialized to the correct value to begin with. Use:

```
base( const char *init_value ) : s(init_value)
{}
```

Now s will be initialized correctly, and there's no need for the operator=() call to reinitialize it.

The current rule also applies to base classes, which are accessible from the derived-class constructor, so they must be initialized before the derived-class constructor is executed. Base classes are initialized before members of the derived class because derived-class members are not visible in the base class. To summarize, objects are initialized in the following order:

- Base classes, in order of declaration.
- Fields, in order of declaration.

Only then is the derived-class constructor executed.

There's one final caveat. Note that the order of declaration controls the order of initialization. The order in which items appear in the member-initialization list is immaterial. Moreover, the order of declaration shouldn't be considered immutable. For example, you might change the order in which fields are declared. Consider this class definition in a *.h* file somewhere:

```
class wilma
{
    int y;
    int x;
public;
    wilma( int ix );
};
```

Here's the constructor definition, in a *.c* file:

```
wilma::wilma( int ix ) : y(ix * 10), x(y + 1)
{}
```

Now suppose that some maintenance programmer comes along and alphabetizes the fields, swapping the order of x and y. The constructor doesn't work any more: x is initialized first because it comes first in the class definition, and it's initialized to y+1, but y is uninitialized.

Fix the code by not assuming anything about initialization order:

```
wilma::wilma( int ix ) : y(ix * 10), x((ix * 10) + 1)
{}
```

130. Copy constructors must use member initialization lists.

Derivation also has its problems with respect to copying. A copy constructor is still a constructor, so the issues discussed in the previous rule apply here, too. If the copy constructor doesn't have a member-initialization list, then the default constructor is used for base classes and contained objects. Because the member initialization list is missing in the following copy-constructor definition, the base-class component of the derived-class object is initialized using base(**void**) and the s field is initialized using string::string(**void**):

```
class base
{
public:
    base( void        );                    // default constructor
    base( const base &r );                  // copy constructor
    const base &operator=( const base &r );
};

class derived
{
    string s;   // class has a copy constructor
public:
    derived( const derived &r )
};

derived::derived( const derived &r )
{}
```

Use the following to guarantee that the string field and the base-class component of the derived-class object are copied too:

```
derived::derived( const derived &r ) : base(r), s(r.s)
{}
```

131. Derived classes should usually define a copy constructor and
   operator=().

There's another copy-related problem under derivation. In one part of the ARM,[10] the document says unequivocally: "constructors and the operator=() function are not inherited." Later on in the same document, however, it says that there are situations where the compiler can't generate a copy

---

[10] Ellis and Stroustroup's *The Annotated C++ Reference Manual* (Reading: Addison Wesley, 1990), which is used as the base document by the ISO/ANSI C++ committee.

constructor or `operator=()` function that chains correctly to the base-class function. Because, there is no practical difference between an inherited `operator=()` and a generated `operator=()` that does nothing but call the base-class function, this ambiguity has caused a lot of grief.

I've seen two completely incompatible behaviors in compilers faced with this dilemma. Some compilers "do it right" in that compiler-generated copy constructors and `operator=()` functions chain automatically to base-class (and contained object) constructors and `operator=()` functions.[11] This is the way that most people assume that the language works. In other words, there are no problems with the following code:

```
class base
{
public:
    base( const base &r );
    const base &operator=( const base &r );
};

class derived : public base
{
    string s;
    // no operator=() or copy constructor
};

derived x;
derived y = x;   // calls base-class  copy constructor to copy base-class.
                 // also calls string copy constructor to copy the s field.
x = y;           // calls base-class  operator=()     to copy base-class.
                 // also calls string operator=()     to copy the s field.
```

If all compilers worked this way, there'd be no problem. Unfortunately, some compilers take the "are not inherited" directive at face value. The code just presented won't work with these compilers. In these compilers, the compiler-generated derived-class copy constructor and `operator=()` function act as if the base-class (and contained-object) equivalents just don't exist. In other words, the *default* constructor—the one with no arguments—is called to copy the base-class component, and a memberwise copy—which might just be a `memcpy()`—is used for the field. My understanding of the new-and-improved draft ISO/ANSI C++ standard is that this behavior is not correct, but for the time being, you have to assume the worst to guarantee portability. Consequently, it's probably a good idea to always put into a derived class a copy constructor and `operator=()` function that explicitly chain to their base-class counterparts. Here's a worst-case implementation of the earlier derived class:

---

[11] Of course, copy constructors and `operator=()` functions that you (as compared to the compiler) provide never chain automatically to their base-class counterparts.

```
class derived : public base
{
    string s;
public:
    derived( const derived &r );
    const derived &operator=( const derived &r );
};
//------------------------------------------------------------
derived::derived( const derived &r ) : base(r), s(r.s)
{}
//------------------------------------------------------------
const derived &derived::operator=( const derived &r )
{
    (* (base*)this) = r;
    s = r.s;
}
```

The member-initialization list in the copy constructor was described earlier. The following excerpt from the `operator=()` function needs some explaining:

```
(* (base*)this) = r;
```

The `this` pointer points at the entire current object, `(base*)this` converts it into a pointer to the base-class component of the current object. `(*(base*)this)` is the object, and `(*(base*)this)=r` passes that object an `=r` message, calling the base-class `operator=()` to overwrite information in the current object from the right operand. You could replace this code with:

```
base::operator=( r );
```

but I've seen compilers reject this statement when the base class did not have an explicitly declared `operator=()` function. The first form works whether or not there's an explicitly declared `operator=()`. (You'll get default, memberwise copy if not.)

132. Constructors not suitable for type conversion should have two or more arguments.

C++ uses constructors for type conversion. For example, the `char*` constructor on line nine of Listing 7 on page 111 also handles the following cast operation:

```
char *pchar = "abcd"
(string) pchar;
```

Remember, a cast is a runtime operator that creates a temporary of the required type and initializes it from the argument. When a class is involved, a constructor is used to do the initialization. This conversion is also used implicitly. The following code works fine because the `char*` string constant is converted silently to a `string` in order to be passed to `f()`:

```
f( const string &s );
//...
f( "doo wha ditty" );
```

The problem is that we sometimes don't want to permit a constructor to be used for implicit type conversion. Consider the following array container that supports an `int` constructor that specifies the array size:

```
class array
{
    //...
public:
    array( int initial_size );
};
```

You probably don't want the following to work, however:

```
f( const array &a );
//...
f( isupper(*str) );
```

(The call passes f() an empty one-element array if *str is upper case or a zero-element array if it's lower case).

The only way to suppress this behavior is to add a second argument to the constructor, because multiple-argument constructors are never used implicitly:

```
class array
{
    //...
public:
    enum bogus { set_size_to };
    array( bogus, int initial_size );
};

array  ar( array::set_size_to, 128 );
```

This is really ugly, but we've no choice. Note that I've not given the bogus argument a name because it's not used for anything other than selecting the function.

133. Use instance counts for class-level initialization.

A few sections back, I discussed using a static global instance count to control library-level initializations. In C++, we have better options because we can use a class definition to limit scope:

```
class window
{
    static int num_windows;
public:
    window();
    ~window();
};

int window::num_windows = 0;

window::window()
{
    if( ++num_windows == 1 )            // have just created first window
        initialize_video_system();
}

window::~window()
{
    if( --num_windows == 0 )            // have just destroyed last window
        shut_down_video_system();
}
```

Finally, an instance count can also be used as a number-of-times-called count to force subroutine-level initialization:

```
f()
{
    static int have_been_called = 0;
    if( !have_been_called )
    {
        have_been_called = 1;
        do_one_time_initializations();
    }
}
```

134. Avoid two-part initialization.

135. C++ wrappers around existing interfaces rarely work well.

Generally, a variable should be initialized at declaration time. Separating the initialization from the declaration is sometimes necessitated by bad design in code that you didn't write, as in the following fragment, written to run under the Microsoft-Foundation-Class (MFC) library:

```
f( CWnd *win )   // CWnd is a window
{
    // The following line loads "buf" with the window caption
    // (the text in the title bar):

    char buf[80]; /* = */ win->GetWindowText(buf, sizeof(buf));
    //...
}
```

Because I must do the initialization with an explicit function call, I've deliberately broken my one-statement-per-line rule in order to at least get the declaration and initialization on the same line.

There are several problems here, the first being bad design of the CWnd class (which represents a window). Because a window has a "text" attribute that holds the caption, you *should* be able to access the attribute like this:

```
CString caption = win->caption();
```

and you should be able to modify the attribute like this:

```
win->caption() = "new contents";
```

but you can't do that with the current implementation.

The main problem is that the Foundation-Class library wasn't designed in an object oriented way—starting with the objects and deciding what messages have to be passed between them and what attributes they have. Instead, Microsoft's designers started with an existing procedural interface (the C application-programming interface [API] to Windows) and put a C++ wrapper around it, thereby perpetuating all the problems of the existing interface. Because the C API has a function called GetWindowText(), the designers mindlessly mimicked this call with a member function in their CWnd wrapper. They did kludge the following call onto the interface:

```
CString str;
win->GetWindowText( str );
```

but this is not a solution for two reasons: Two-part initialization is still required and the argument is a reference-output.

The main lesson is that procedural designs are radically different in structure from object-oriented designs. It's usually not possible to move code from one design to another without major rewriting. Just wrapping C++ classes around a procedural design does not make that design object oriented.

It's instructive, I think, to grope around looking for a solution to the current problem using C++, but I'll warn you that there is no good solution here (other than redesigning the class library). My first attempt to put a layer around CWnd is in Listing 11.

The auxiliary class (window::caption) is needed to permit win->text()="new caption". The text() call returns a caption object, which is then passed the = message.

The main problem with Listing 11 is that the Foundation-Class library has many classes that derive from CWnd, and the interface implemented in class window won't be reflected in the interface to these other CWnd derivatives. C++ is a compiled language, so it's not possible to insert a class into the middle of a class hierarchy without changing the source code.

Listing 12 defines another solution of sorts. I've split out the window::caption class into a standalone class that's attached to a window when it's initialized. Use it like this:

```
f(CWnd *win)
{
    caption cap( win )

    CString s = cap;        // conversion to CString is supported.
    cap = "New Caption";    // uses operator=(CString&)
}
```

I don't like the way that changing a caption also changes the window to which the caption is attached in this last example. The hidden connection between two objects could, itself, be a source of misunderstanding, being too much like a macro side effect. Be that as it may, Listing 12 does solve the initialization problem.

Listing 11. A layer around CWnd: attempt one.

```
1   class window : public CWnd
2   {
3   public:
4       class caption
5       {
6           CWnd *target_window;
7
8       private: friend class window;
9           caption( CWnd *p ) : target_window(p) {}
10
11      public:
12          operator CString          ( void                 ) const;
13          const caption &operator=( const CString &s  );
14      };
15
16      caption text( void );
17  };
18  //-------------------------------------------
19  caption window..text( void )
20  {
21      return caption( this );
22  }
23  //-------------------------------------------
24  window::caption::operator CString( void ) const
25  {
26      CString output;
27      target_window->GetWIndowText( output );
28      return output;               // returns a copy
29  }
30  //-------------------------------------------
31  const caption &window::caption::operator=( const CString &s )
32  {
33      target_window->SetWindowText( s );
34      return *this;
35  }
```

Listing 12. A Caption Object

```
1   class caption
2   {
3       CWnd target_window;
4   public:
5       window_text( CWnd *win ) : target_window( win ) {};
6
7       operator const CString( void );
8       const CString &operator=( const CString &r );
9   };
10
11  inline caption::operator CString( void );
12  {
13      CString output;
14      target_window->GetWindowText( output );
15      return output;
16  }
17
18  inline const CString &caption::operator= ( const CString &s )
19  {
20      // returns a CString (rather than a "caption") so that
21      //      a = b = "abc"
22      // will work
23
24      target_window->SetWindowText( s );
25      return s;
26  }
```

Part 8.E. Virtual Functions

Virtual functions give a derived-class object the ability to modify behavior defined at the base class level (or to provide some capability that the base class needs but can't implement, usually because the information needed to do the implementation is declared at the derived-class level). Virtual functions are central to object-oriented design because they let you define a general-purpose base class without needing to know specifics that can be provided only by the derived class. You can write code that thinks it's manipulating base-class objects but that actually manipulates derived-class objects at runtime. You can write code to put an object into a generic data_structure, for example, but at runtime actually do the insert into a tree or a linked_list (classes that derive from data_structure). This is such a fundamental object-oriented operation that C++ code that doesn't use virtual functions is probably not designed properly.

136. Virtual functions are those functions that you can't write at the base-class level.

Virtual functions exist for two purposes. First, virtual functions define capabilities that all derived-classes must have, but which can't be implemented at the base-class level. For example, you could say that all shape objects must be capable of printing themselves. You can't write a print() function at the base-class level because the geometric information is stored in the derived classes (circle, line, polygon, etc.). So you make print() virtual in the base class and actually define the function in the derived class.

The second purpose is a workhorse virtual function. Take our storable class as an example. To store an object in a sorted data structure, a storable object has to be able to compare itself to another storable object. That is, the database function will have code like this:

```
add( storable *insert )
{
    storable *object_already_in_database;
    //...
    if( object_already_in_database->cmp(insert) < 0 )
        // object_already_in_database < insert
}
```

The storable object, again, can't define a cmp() function because the information that needs to be compared (the key) is in the derived-class object, not in the storable base class. So you make the function virtual in the storable class and provide it in the derived class. These workhorse functions will never be public, by the way.

137. A virtual function isn't virtual when called from a constructor or destructor.

This isn't so much rule but a statement of fact, although it comes as a surprise to many. Base classes are initialized before derived classes. Also, derived-class functions presumably access derived-class data; otherwise there'd be no point in putting the function in the derived class. If a base-class constructor could call a derived-class function through the virtual-function mechanism, the function could effectively use uninitialized derived-class data fields.

Just to make things crystal clear, lets look at what's happening under the hood. The virtual function mechanism is implemented by means of a table of function pointers. When you declare a class such as the following one:

```
class storable
{
    int stuff;
public:
    storable( void );

    virtual void print( void            );
    virtual void virtf( void            );
    virtual int  cmp  ( const storable &r ) = 0;

    int nonvirtual( void );
};

    storable::storable  ( void ) { stuff = 0;                        }
void storable::print    ( void ) { /* print debugging stuff */ }
void storable::virtf    ( void ) { /* do something */          }
int  storable::nonvirtual( void ) {                             }
```

The underlying class definition (as generated by the compiler) might look like this:

```
int _storable__print    ( storable *this ) { /*...*/ }
int _storable__virtf     ( storable *this ) { /*...*/ }
int _storable__nonvirtual( storable *this ) { /*...*/ }

typedef void (*_vtab[])(...);              // array of function pointers

_vtab _storable__vtab
{
    _storable__print,
    _storable__virtf,
    NULL                       // place holder for compare function
};

typedef struct storable
{
    _storable__vtab *_vtable;
    int stuff;
}
storable;

_storable__ctor( void )          // constructor
{
    _vtable = _storable__vtab;  // Compiler adds this line
    stuff   = 0;                // This line came from source code.
}
```

When you call a nonvirtual function, using code like this:

```
storable *p;
p->nonvirtual();
```

the compiler effectively generates:

```
_storable__nonvirtual( p )
```

When you call a virtual function like this:

```
p->print();
```

you get something very different:

```
( p->_vtable[0] )( p );
```

It's this indirection through the table that makes virtual functions work. When you call a derived-class function through a base-class pointer, the compiler doesn't even know it's looking at a derived class function. For example, here's a derived-class definition at the source-code level:

```
class employee: public storable
{
    int derived_stuff;
    //...
public:
    virtual int cmp( const storable &r );
};

/*virtual*/ int employee::print( const storable &r ) { }
/*virtual*/ int employee::cmp  ( const storable &r ) { }
```

Here's what the compiler will do with it:

```
int _employee__print( employee *this                       ){ /*...*/ }
int _employee__cmp  ( employee *this, const storable *ref_r ){ /*...*/ }

_vtab _employee_vtable =
{
    _employee__print,
    _storable_virtf,    // There's no derived-class override, so use
                        // a pointer to the base-class function.
    _employee_cmp
};

typedef struct employee
{
    _vtab *_vtable;     // Compiler-generated field.
    int stuff;          // Base-class field.
    int derived_stuff;  // Field added in derived-class declaration.
}
employee;

_employee__ctor( employee *this )    // Default constructor, generated by
{                                    // the compiler.
    _storable_ctor();                // Base classes are initialized first.
    _vtable = _employee_vtable;      // Set up virtual-function table.
}
```

The compiler has overwritten those slots in the virtual-function table that represent derived-class overrides of virtual functions. The virtual function that has not been overridden in the derived class (virtf remains initialized to the base-class function).

When you create an object at runtime with:

```
storable *p = new employee();
```

the compiler effectively generates:

```
storable *p;
p = (storable *)malloc( sizeof(employee) );
_employee_ctor( p );
```

The call to the _employee_ctor() first initializes the base-class component by calling _storable_ctor(), which sets up the virtual function table to its own table and executes. Then control transfers back to _employee_ctor() and overwrites the virtual-function-table pointer to point at the derived-class table.

Note that, even though p now points at an employee, the code p->print() generates exactly the same code as before:

```
( p->_vtable[0] )( p );
```

Now, however, p points at a derived-class object, so the derived-class version of print() is called (because _vtable in a derived-class object points at the derived class table). It's critical that the two print() functions be in the same slot in their relative tables, but the compiler makes sure that this works.

Returning to the main point of the current rule, the initialization order is important when considering how constructors work. The base-class constructor is called by the derived-class constructor before it does anything else. Because _vtable points at the base-class virtual function table when in the base-class constructor, you'll end up getting base-class virtual functions when you call them. A print call in the base class constructor still gets:

```
( this->_vtable[0] )( p );
```

but _vtable points at the base-class table and _vtable[0] points at the base-class function. The same call in the derived-class constructor would get the derived-class version of print(), because _vtable will have been overwritten by a pointer to the derived-class table by the time print() was called.

Though I haven't shown it previously, the same thing goes on in a destructor. The first thing a destructor does is point _vtable at the table for its own class. Only then does it execute the code that you provide. A derived-class destructor calls the base-class destructor on the way out (at the very bottom of the function—after the user-supplied code is executed).

138. Do not call pure virtual functions from constructors.

This rule is mandated by the behavior just discussed. A "pure" virtual function definition (one with an =0 instead of a body) causes a NULL to be put into the base-class virtual-function table in place of the usual function pointer. (In the case of a "pure" virtual function, there is no real function to point to.) If you call a pure virtual function from a constructor, you'll be using the base-class table and will effectively be calling a function through a NULL pointer. You'll get a core dump on a UNIX machine and a "General Protection Fault" in a Windows system, but MS-DOS does just what you ask and tries to execute the code at memory-location 0 as if it were legitimate.

139. Destructors should always be `virtual`.

Consider this code:

```
class base
{
    char *p;

    ~base(){ p = new char[SOME_SIZE]; }
     base(){ delete p;                }
};

class derived : public base
{
    char *dp;

    ~derived(){ dp = new char[SOME_SIZE]; }
     derived(){ delete dp;                }
};
```

Now consider this call:

```
base *p = new derived;
//...
delete p;
```

Remember, the compiler doesn't know that p actually points at a derived-class object. It assumes that p points at the declared type, a base. Consequently, the `delete p` effectively turns into:

```
_base__destructor(p);
free(p);
```

The derived-class destructor is never called. If you redefine the classes to make the destructor virtual:

```
virtual ~base(){ /*...*/ }
```

the compiler accesses the destructor through the virtual-function table, just like any other virtual function. Because the destructor is now `virtual`, `delete p` now generates:

```
( p->_vtable[DESTRUCTOR_SLOT] )(p);
```

Because p points at a derived-class object, you get the derived-class destructor, which chains to the base-class destructor when it's done with the derived-class component.

140. Base-class functions that have the same name as derived-class functions generally should be virtual.

Remember, a public function is a message handler. If the base class and the derived class both have message handlers with the same name, you're saying that the derived-class object has to do something different from a base-class object to handle the same message. The whole point of derivation is to be able to write general code in terms of base-class objects, and have that code work even if it's dealing with derived-class objects. Consequently the message should be handled by the derived-class function, not the base-class function.

The one common exception to this rule is an operator overload where the base class might define some set of overloads and the derived class wants to add an *additional* overload (as compared to changing the behavior of a base-class overload). Though the overload functions in the two classes will have the same names, they'll most certainly have different signatures, so they can't be virtual.

141. Don't make a function `virtual` unless you want the derived class to get control of it.

I've read that you should make all member functions virtual "just in case." This is not good advice. You certainly don't want a derived class to get control of all your workhorse functions; otherwise, you'd never be able to write reliable code.

142. `protected` functions should usually be `virtual`.

One mitigating factor in the base-class/derived-class coupling situation described earlier is that a C++ derived-class object hardly ever needs to send a message to its base-class component. The derived class inherits functionality (and members) from, and usually adds functionality (and members) to, the base class, but the derived class doesn't often call base-class functions. (A derived class should *never* access base-class data, of course.) One exception is virtual functions, which can be seen as a means of changing base-class behavior. Messages are often passed from a derived-class override to the equivalent base-class function. That is, a derived-class virtual override often chains to the base-class function that it is overriding. For example, the MFC's CDialog class implements a Windows dialog box (a kind of data-entry window). The class provides a virtual function called OnOk(), which shuts down the dialog box when a user clicks the button labeled "OK." You define a dialog box of your own by deriving from CDialog, and you might provide an override of OnOk() that does data validation before allowing the dialog box to shut down. Your override chains to the base-class function to actually do the shutting down:

```
class mydialog : public CDialog
{
    //...
private:
    virtual OnOk( void );
};

/*virtual*/ mydialog::OnOk( void );
{
    if( data_is_valid() )
        CDialog::OnOk();        // Send message to base class
    else
        beep();                 // typically informative Windows error message
}
```

The OnOk() function is private in the derived class because nobody will send an OnOk() message to a mydialog object. The base class's OnOk() can't be private because you need to chain to it from the derived-class override. You don't want CDialog::OnOk() to be public because, again, nobody should be sending an OnOk() message to a CDialog object. So, you make it protected. The derived-class override can now chain to OnOk(), but the function isn't externally accessible.

It's not a good idea to use protected to provide a secret interface to the base class that only the derived class can use because this can hide a coupling relationship. Though such a protected function is occasionally the only way to do things, the normal public interface is usually a better choice.

Note that this rule doesn't flip around. Though `protected` functions should usually be `virtual`, many `virtual` functions are `public`.

143. Beware of casts: C++ issues.

C casts were discussed earlier, and casts cause problems in C++ too. In C++, you also have the problem of down casting—the casting of a base-class pointer or reference to the derived class. The problem usually appears in virtual-function overrides because the derived-class function signature must exactly match that of the base class. Consider this code:

```cpp
class base
{
public:
    virtual int operator==( const base &r ) = 0;
};

class derived : public base
{
    char *key;

public:
    virtual int operator==( const base &r )
    {
        return strcmp(key, ((const derived &)r).key ) == 0;
    }
};
```

Unfortunately, there's no guarantee that the incoming `r` argument actually references a derived-class object. It can't reference a base-class object because of the pure virtual function; you can't instantiate a `base` object. It could, however, reference an object of some other class that derives from `base` but wasn't of class `derived`. Given the earlier definition, the following code doesn't work:

```cpp
class other_derived : public base
{
    int key;
    //...
};

f()
{
    derived         dobj;
    other_derived   other;

    if( derived == other_derived )
        id_be_shocked();
}
```

The ISO/ANSI C++ committee has introduced a runtime typing mechanism that solves this problem, but at this writing many compilers don't support it. The proposed syntax looks like this:

```
class derived : public base
{
    char *key;

public:
    virtual int operator==( const base &r )
    {
        derived *p = dynamic_cast<derived *>( &r );

        return !p ? 0 : strcmp(key, ((const derived &)r).key )==0 ;
    }
};
```

The `dynamic_cast<t>` evaluates to 0 if the operand cannot safely be converted to type `t`, otherwise it does the conversion.

This rule is also a good demonstration of why you don't want all classes in your hierarchy to derive from a common `object` class. It's almost impossible to use arguments of class `object` directly because the `object` class itself defines almost no functionality. You find yourself constantly casting `object` pointers into whatever type the incoming argument actually is. This cast is dangerous Without runtime typing because you might be converting to the wrong type. The cast is ugly even with runtime typing, adding unnecessary clutter to the code.

144. Don't call constructors from `operator=()`

Though this rule talks about assignment overloads, it's really addressing a virtual-function problem. It's a temptation to implement `operator=()` like this:

```
class some_class
{
public:

    virtual
    ~some_class( void            );
     some_class( void            );
     some_class( const some_class &r );

     const some_class &operator=( const some_class &r );
};

const some_class &operator=( const some_class &r )
{
    if( this != &r )
    {
        this->~some_class();
        new(this) some_class(r);
    }
    return *this;
}
```

This variant of `new` initializes the object pointed to by `this` as a `some_class` object, in this case using the copy constructor because of the `r` argument.[12]

There are several reasons not to do the foregoing. First, it doesn't work under derivation. When you define:

```
class derived : public some_class
{
public:
    ~derived();

    // Assume that compiler-generated operator=()
    // chains to base-class operator=().
}
```

Because the base-class destructor is (correctly) defined as `virtual`, the earlier base-class call to:

```
this->~some_class()
```

calls the derived-class constructor, so you'll destroy a lot more than you had intended. You can try to fix this problem by changing the destructor call to:

```
this->some_class::~some_class();
```

An explicit call-out of a class name—the `some_class::` in this example—suppresses the virtual function mechanism. The function is called as if it weren't virtual.

The destructor isn't the only problem. Consider a simple assignment of derived-class objects:

```
derived d1, d2;
d1 = d2;
```

The derived-class `operator=()` (whether or not it's compiler generated) chains to the base class `operator=()`, which, in the current case, uses `operator new()` to explicitly call the base-class constructor. A constructor does a lot more than what you can see in the definition, however. In particular, it initializes the virtual-function-table pointer to point at the table for its class. In the current example, before the assignment, the `vtable` pointer points at the derived-class table. After the assignment, the `vtable` pointer points at the *base class* table; it's been reinitialized by the constructor call implicit in the `new` invocation in the `operator=()` overload.

So, calling constructors in an `operator=()` function just doesn't work if there's a virtual-function table. Because you might or might not know what your base-class definitions look like, you must assume that a virtual-function table is there, so don't do it.

The best way to eliminate duplicate code in an `operator=()` is with a common workhorse function:

---

12 Some compilers actually permit an explicit constructor call, so you could possibly do the same thing as follows:

```
const some_class &operator=( const some_class &r )
{
    if( this != &r )
    {
        this->~some_class();
        this->some_class::some_class( r );
    }
}
```

This behavior is nonstandard, however.

```
class some_class
{
    void create ( void              );
    void create ( const some_class &r   );
    void destroy( void              );
public:

    virtual
    ~some_class( void ){ destroy(); }
     some_class( void ){ create (); }

     const some_class &operator=( const some_class &r );
};

inline const some_class &some_class::operator=( const some_class &r )
{
    destroy();
    create( r );
}

inline  some_class::some_class( void )
{
    create();
}

~some_class::some_class( void )
{
    destroy();
}
```

Part 8.F. Operator Overloads

145. An operator is an abbreviation (no surprises).

An operator is not an arbitrary squiggle that means whatever you want it to mean. It's an abbreviation for an English word. For example, the symbol + mean "add," so you shouldn't overload `operator+()` to do anything else. Though the obvious applies here (you can define a+b to subtract b from a, but you shouldn't), I'm really talking about more-creative problems.

You can reasonably argue that, when you concatenate, you are "adding" one string to the end of another, so an overload of + for concatenation might be reasonable. You can also argue that it's reasonable to use relational operators to do lexicographic ranking in a `string` class, so overloads of <, ==, and so forth, are probably okay as well. You cannot argue reasonably that - or * have any meaning with respect to strings.

Another good example of how not to do things is C++'s *iostream* interface. Using shift (<<) to mean "output" is nonsensical. Your C output function is called `printf()`, not `shiftf()`. I understand that Stroustrup chose a shift because it's analogous to various UNIX shells' I/O redirection mechanisms, but this rational doesn't really hold up under scrutiny. Stroustrup is assuming that all C++ programmers understand UNIX-style redirection, but the concept doesn't exist in some operating systems; Microsoft Windows is an example. Also, to make the analogy complete, > should be overloaded to perform an overwrite operation, and >> should append. The fact that > and >> have different precedence levels makes implementing this behavior awkward, however. Matters are made worse by the fact that the shift operators are at the wrong precedence level. A statement like `cout << x += 1` doesn't work as you expect because << is higher precedence than +=, so it is interpreted as `(cout<<x) += 1`, which is illegal. C++ needs the extensibility provided by the iostream system, but it should get it by introducing "input" and "output" operators that have the lowest precedence of any operators in the language.

An analogy to the shift-as-output problem can be found in hardware design. Most hardware designers would be happy using + to mean OR and * to mean AND because that notation is used in many hardware-design environments. An overload of `operator+()` that did an OR operations is obviously undesirable in C++, however. By the same token << means "shift" in C and C++; it doesn't mean "output."

As a final example of the problem, I've sometimes seen implementations of a "set" class define | and & to mean "union" and "intersection." This might make perfect sense to a mathematician, who is familiar with this style of notation, but it is neither a C nor C++ idiom, so it will be unfamiliar to your average C++ programmer (and thus hard to maintain). An ampersand is an abbreviation for AND; you should not assign an arbitrary meaning to it. There's absolutely nothing wrong with `a.Union(b)` or `a.intersect(b)`. (You can't say `a.union(b)`, with a lower-case "u," because `union` is a keyword.)

146. Use operator overloads only to define operations for which there is a C analog (no surprises).

Operator overloading was put into the language primarily so that you can integrate an arithmetic type that you invent into the existing C arithmetic system. The mechanism was never intended to be a means for extending that system. Consequently, it's best to use operator overloading only when using classes to implement an arithmetic type.

Nonetheless, it's also reasonable to use operator overloads anywhere that a C analogy is unremarkable. For example, most classes will overload assignment. Overloads of `operator==()` and `operator!=()` are also reasonable with most classes.

A less obvious (and more controversial) example is an "iterator" class. An *iterator* is means of visiting every member of a data structure, and it's used almost exactly as if it were a pointer to an array. For example, you can iterate across an array, visiting every element, in C as follows:

```
string array[ size ];
string *p = array;

for( int i = size; --i >= 0 ; )
    visit( *p++ );                    // visit() is passed a string.
```

A C++ analog might look like this (`keys` is a tree whose nodes have `string` keys; any other data structure would do, here):

```
tree<string>  keys;      // binary tree with nodes having string keys
iterator p  = keys;
//...
for( int i = keys.size(); --i >= 0 ; )
    visit( *p++ );                    // visit() is passed a string
```

In other words, you treat a tree as if it were an array and can iterate across it with an iterator that works like a pointer to an element. Because the `iterator` (p) behaves exactly like a C pointer, the no surprises rule is not violated.

147. Once you overload an operation, you must overload all similar operations.

This rule is a continuation of the previous rule. Once you say that "an iterator works just like a pointer," it really must work just like a pointer. The example in the previous rule used only the overloads of `*` and `++` but my real-world implementation of an iterator completes the analogy by supporting *every* pointer operation. Table 4 shows various possibilities (`t` is a tree and `ti` is a tree iterator). `*++p` and `*p++` both have to work, etc. In the earlier example, I would also overload `operator[]` and (unary) `operator*()` in the `tree` class to make the tree-as-array analogy hold everywhere. You get the idea.

One problem here is `operator==()` and `operator!=()`, which superficially seem to make sense in situations where other relational operators are meaningless. For example, you might consider using `==` to test two circles for equivalence, but does "equivalence" mean "at the same location having the same radius" or does it just mean "having the same radius?" Overloads of other relational operators like `<` or `<=` are even more dubious because their meaning is not immediately apparent. It's best to avoid operator overloading entirely if any ambiguity of meaning exists.

Table 4. Operator overloads in an iterator.

Operation	Description
`ti = t;`	*Reinitialize to start of the sequence*
`--ti;`	*Return to previous node*
`ti += i;`	*Seek forward i nodes*
`ti -= i;`	*Seek backwards i nodes*
`ti +  i;`	*Evaluates to another temporary-variable iterator, initialized to the*
`ti -  i;`	*Indicated offset from ti.*
`ti[i];`	*Node at offset i from the current position*
`ti[-i];`	*Node at offset -i from the current position*
`t2 = ti;`	*Copy position from one iterator to another.*
`t2 - ti;`	*Distance between two elements addressed by separate iterators*
`ti->msg();`	*Send a message to the node.*
`(*ti).msg();`	*Send a message to the node.*

118. Operator overloads should work exactly like they would in C.

The main new issue here is lvalues and rvalues. Lvalues are easy to describe in C++: They're just references. The C compiler, when evaluating expressions, processes the operators one at a time, with the processing order determined by associativity and precedence rules. Each stage in the evaluation uses a temporary variable generated by the previous operation. Some operators generate "rvalues," actual objects that actually hold a value. Other operators generate "lvalues," references to objects. ("L" and "r," are used by the way, because in the expression l=r, the thing on the left of the = generates an lvalue. The thing on the right forms an rvalue.)

You can minimize surprises to your readers by making your operator overload functions work identically to their C equivalents in terms of what they can do. Here's how the C operators work and how to mimic the behavior:

- Assignment operations (=, +=, -=, etc.) and autoincrement and autodecrement operators (++, --) require lvalue operands for the target—the thing being modified. Think of ++ as equivalent to +=1 to see why it's in the same category as assignment.

  In a member-function operator overload, this *is effectively an lvalue, so there's nothing to worry about. At the global level, the left operand of binary assignment-operator overload (and the only operand to a unary assignment-operator overload) must be a reference.*

- All other operators can take either lvalue or rvalue operands.

  Use a reference to a const *object for all operands. (You could also pass operands by value, but that's usually less efficient.)*

- Variable names of aggregates (arrays) generate rvalues—temporary variables of type pointer-to-first-element, initialized to point at the first element. Note that the notion that you can't increment an array name because it's a constant is actually not correct. You can't increment an array name because it's an rvalue, and all the increment operators require lvalue operands.

Variable names for nonaggregates generate lvalues.

The *, ->, ., and [] operators generate lvalues when the referenced thing is not an aggregate, otherwise they work like aggregate-variable names. If y is an array x->y generates an lvalue that references the field. If y is not an array x->y generates an rvalue that references the first cell of the array.

*In C++, overloads of * and [] should return references to the indicated object.* operator-> *is weird. The rules essentially force you to use it the same way you would in C.* -> *is treated as a unary operator with the operand to it's left. The overload function must return a pointer to something that has fields in it—a* struct, class, *or* union. *The compiler will then use the field to get the lvalue or rvalue. You can't overload a* ..

- All other operands generate rvalues.

The equivalent operator overloads should return objects. They should not return references or pointers.

149. It's best for a binary-operator overload to be an `inline` alias for a cast.

This is one that will change as compilers improve in quality. Consider the following, easy-to-understand augmentation to the string class in Listing 7 on page 111.

```
class string
{
    enum special_ { special };
    string( special_ ){};        // does nothing.
    //...
public:
    const string operator+( const string &r ) const;
    //...
};
//------------------------------------------------------------
const string::operator+( const string &r ) const
{
    string tmp( special );        // make an empty object

    tmp.buf = new char[ strlen(buf) + strlen(r.buf) + 1 ];
    strcpy( tmp.buf, buf    );
    strcat( tmp.buf, r.buf );
    return tmp;
}
```

Many compilers generate rather inefficient code when given the foregoing. The tmp object must be initialized with a constructor call; it's not a very expensive one here, but it usually is much higher overhead. tmp must be destroyed with a matching destructor call when the function returns. The copy constructor must be called to process the return, and this object will have to be destroyed, too.

You can sometimes improve this behavior by making the operator-overload an `inline` alias for a cast operation:

```
class string
{
    string(const char *left, const char *right );
public:
    const string string::operator+( const string &r ) const;
};
//----------------------------------------------------------
string::string(const char *left, const char *right )
{
    buf = new char[ strlen(left) + strlen(right) + 1 ];
    strcpy( buf, left  );
    strcat( buf, right );
}
//----------------------------------------------------------
inline const string::operator+( const string &r ) const
{
    return string(buf, r.buf);
}
```

Compilers that do better here effectively treat.

```
string s1, s2;
s1 + s2;
```

as if you had said the following (you can't do this yourself because `buf` is `private`):

```
string(s1.buf,s2.buf)
```

The net result is elimination of the copy-constructor call implicit in the `return` statement of the first implementation.

Constructors used in this way are often declared `private`, as is the case here, because the user would not normally need to access them directly.

150. Don't go bonkers with type-conversion operators.

151. Do all type conversions with constructors if possible.

It's a common error among new C++ programmers to go nuts with type conversions. You feel that you have to provide conversions from every type in the system to your new class and vice versa. This can lead to code like the following:

```
class riches
{
public:
    riches( const rags &r );
};

class rags
{
public:
    operator riches( void );
};
```

The problem is that both functions define a conversion from `rags` to `riches`. The following code generates a "hard error" (one that renders the compilation invalid) because the compiler doesn't know whether to convert `rags` to `riches` using the constructor in class `riches` or the operator overload in class `rags`; they both claim to do the job:

```
rags horatio_alger;

riches bill_gates = (riches) horatio_alger;
```

This problem is usually not so obvious. For example, if you define too many conversions:

```
class some_class
{
public:
    operator int          (void);
    operator const char * (void);
};
```

a simple statement like:

```
some_class x;
cout << x;
```

won't work. The problem is that class `stream` defines both of the following:

```
ostream &ostream::operator<<( int x      );
ostream &ostream::operator<<( const char *s );
```

Because both conversions are available, the compiler doesn't know which one to call.

It's best to do all type conversion with constructors, and define the minimum set necessary. For example, If you have a conversion from `double`, you don't need `int`, `long`, and so forth because the normal C type-conversion rules are still applied by the compiler in order to call your constructor.

Part 8.G. Memory Management

152. Use new/delete rather than malloc()/free().

There's no guarantee that operator new() calls malloc() to get its memory. It could implement its own memory manager. Consequently, it's a hard-to-detect error to pass free() memory that came from new (and vice versa).

Avoid the problem by always using new and delete when you're writing C++. Among other things, this means that you shouldn't use strdup() or any other function that hides a malloc() call.

153. All memory allocated in a constructor should be freed in the destructor.

Not doing this is usually a bug, but I've seen code that did it on purpose. The code in question actually violated another rule: Don't allow public access to private data. A member function not only returned an internal pointer that addressed new memory, but the class expected the calling function to pass that pointer to delete. This is a bad idea on both counts; a memory leak is just too easy.

On the "bug" front, it helps to put the constructor and destructor functions physically close to each other in the .cpp file to make it easier to notice when you blow it.

154. Local overloads of new and delete are dangerous.

The main problem here is that overloads of new and delete defined as class members follow different rules than do the global-level overloads. The local overload is used only when you allocate a single object. The global overload is always used when you allocate an array. Consequently, this code probably won't work:

```
some_class *p = new some_class[1];   // calls global operator new()
    //...
delete p;                            // calls some_class::operator delete()
```

Remember that these two lines could be in different files.

Part 8.H. Templates

Many problems with templates are really caused by the textbooks, which typically simplify the discussion of templates so much that you end up without a clue about how they should be used. This section addresses common template problems.

155. Use `inline` function templates instead of parameterized macros.

Given the earlier:

```
#define SQUARE(x) ((x) * (x))
```

a:

```
SQUARE(++x)
```

expands to:

```
((++x)*(++x))
```

incrementing x twice. You can't solve this problem in C, but you can in C++. A simple `inline` function works to some extent, in that:

```
inline int square( int x ){ return x * x; }
```

has no side effects. It only accepts `int` arguments, however. A function template that expands to multiple overloads of the `inline` function is a more general solution:

```
template <class type>
inline type square( type x ){ return x * x; }
```

Unfortunately, this works only in simple situations. The following template can't handle the invocation `max(10,10L)` because the argument types aren't the same:

```
template <class type>
inline type max( type x, type y ){ return (x > y) ? x : y; }
```

To handle `max(10,10L)`, you'd have use a prototype to force expansion of a version of `max()` that could do the job:

```
long max( long, long );
```

The prototype forces a template expansion. The compiler is happy to convert the `int` argument to `long` to *call* the function, even though it won't do the conversion to expand the template.

Note that I'm recommending the use of templates here only because `square` is an `inline` function. If it weren't, too much code would be generated for the mechanism to be viable.

156. Always be aware of the size of the expanded template.

Most books demonstrate templates with a simple array container like the one in Listing 13. You can't use derivation here (say, with an `array` base class from which a `int_array` derives). The problem is the `operator[]()` overload. You'd want it to be a virtual function in the base class, then override it in the derived classes, but the signature of the derived-class version would have to differ from the base class signature for this to work. Here, the function definitions would differ only by return type: `int_array::operator[]()` would need to return an `int` reference, `long_array::operator[]()` would need to return a `long` reference, and so forth. Because the return time isn't considered as part of the signature when function-overloads are evaluated, a derivation-based implementation isn't viable. A template is the only solution.

Listing 13. A simple array container.

```
1   template <class type, int size >
2   class array
3   {
4       type array[size];
5   public:
6       class out_of_bounds {};        // thrown when you use an
7                                      // out-of-bounds array index.
8       type &operator[](int index);
9   };
10
11  template <class type, int size >
12  inline type &array<type,size>::operator[](int index)
13  {
14      if( 0 <= index && index < size )
15          return array[ index ]
16      throw out_of_bounds;
17  }
```

The only reason that this definition is practical is that the member function is inline. If it weren't, you could have a massive amount of duplicate code. Remember that all of the following expand out the complete template including all member functions. Because each of the following definitions effectively creates a different type, you'd expand the template four times, generating four identical `operator[]()` functions, one for each template expansion:

```
array<int,10>   ten_element_array;
array<int,11>   eleven_element_array;
array<int,12>   twelve_element_array;
array<int,13>   thirteen_element_array;
```

(`array<int,10>::operator[]()`, `array<int,11>::operator[]()`, and so forth).

The question then is how to minimize this duplicate code. What if we pull the size out of the template, as in Listing 14? The earlier declarations now look like this:

```
array<int>   ten_element_array       (10);
array<int>   eleven_element_array    (11);
array<int>   twelve_element_array    (12);
array<int>   thirteen_element_array  (13);
```

We now have only one class definition (and one version of `operator[]()`), with four instances of the class.

Listing 14. An array template (Pass 2).

```
1    template <class type>
2    class array
3    {
4        type *array;
5        int size;
6    public:
7        virtual ~array( void );
8        array( int size = 128 );
9
10       class out_of_bounds {};        // thrown when you use an
11                                       // out-of-bounds array index.
12       type &operator[](int index);
13   };
14
15   template <class type>
16   array<type>::array( int sz /*= 128*/ ): size(sz)
17                                         , array( new type[ sz ] )
18   {}
19
20   template <class type>
21   array<type>::~array( void )
22   {
23       delete [] array;
24   }
25
26   template <class type>
27   inline type &array<type>::operator[](int index)
28   {
29       if( 0 <= index && index < size )
30           return array[ index ]
31       throw out_of_bounds;
32   }
```

The main disadvantage of this second implementation is that you can't declare a two-dimensional array. The definition in listing 13 allows the following:

```
array< array<int,10>, 20>   ar;
```

(a 20-element array of 10-element arrays). The definition in Listing 14 sizes the array using the constructor, so the best you can get is:

```
array< array<int> >   ar2(20);
```

The inner `array<int>` is created using the default constructor, so it's a 128-element array; we've declared a 20-element array of 128-element arrays.

You can solve this last problem with derivation. Consider the following derived-class definition:

```
template< class type, int size >
class sized_array : public array<type>
{
public:
    sized_array() : array<type>(size) {}
};
```

There's nothing here but a single inline function, so this is a very light class definition; It will not expand the program's size at all, no matter how many times the template is expanded. You can now say:

```
sized_array< sized_array<int,10>, 20>  ar3;
```

to get a 20-element array of 10-element arrays.

157. Class templates should usually define derived classes.

158. Templates do not replace derivation; they automate it.

The main thing to remember about class templates is that they will spawn many class definitions. As in the case every time you have multiple similar class definitions, identical functions should be combined into a common base class.

First, let's look at how *not* to do things. The storable class that I've been using as an example provides a good example. First, let's make a collection object that manages storable objects:

```
class collection
{
    storable *head;
public:
    //...
    storable *find( const storable &a_match_of_this ) const;
};

storable *collection::find( const storable &a_match_of_this ) const
{
    // Send a message to the head-of-list object requesting
    // that it search the list for a match of a_match_of_this;

    return head ? head->find( a_match_of_this )
                : NULL
                ;
}
```

The mechanics of finding things is hidden in storable. You can change the underlying data structure by changing the storable definition, and those changes won't affect the collection implementation at all.

Next, let's implement a storable that uses a simple linked list as its underlying data structure:

```
class storable
{
    storable *next, *prev;

public:
    storable    *find      ( const storable &match_of_this ) const;
    storable    *successor ( void                           ) const;
    virtual int operator== ( const storable &r              ) const;
};

storable *storable::find( const storable &match_of_this ) const;
{
    // Returns a pointer to the first node in the list rooted
    // at myself who has the same key as "r". Typically, a
    // collection object would send this message to the
    // head-of-list object, a pointer to which is stored in
    // the collection class.

    storable *current = this;
    for(; current; current = current->next )
        if( *current == match_of_this )            // found a match
            return current;
}

storable *storable::successor( void ) const
{
    // Returns the next node in sequence.
    return next;
}
```

The operator==() function has to be pure virtual because there's no way to implement it at the storable level. Implementation has to be done in a derived class:[13]

```
class storable_string : public storable
{
    string s;
public:
    virtual int operator==( const storable &r ) const;
    //...
};

virtual int operator==( const storable &r ) const
{
    storable_string *right = dynamic_cast<storable_string *>( &r );

    return right ? (s == r.s) : NULL;
}
```

I've used the proposed ISO/ANSI C++ type-safe down-cast mechanism, here. right is initialized to

---

[13] I'd probably use multiple inheritance in the real world, deriving a class from string. I've used containment here to simplify the example a bit.

NULL if the incoming object (r) is not a storable_string. For example, it could be some other class that derives from storable.

So far, so good. Now for the template-related issues. Somebody who doesn't know what they're doing says: "Oh boy, I can eliminate both the derivation and the need for virtual functions with a template," probably by doing something like this:

```
template <class t_key>
class storable
{
    storable *next, *prev;

    t_key key;

public:
    //...
    storable *find        ( const storable &match_me  ) const;
    storable *successor ( void                         ) const;
    int          operator==( const storable &r         ) const;
    storable
};

template <class t_key>
int storable<t_key>::operator==( const storable<t_key> &r ) const
{
    return key == r.key ;
}

template <class t_key>
storable<t_key> *storable<t_key>::successor( void ) const
{
    return next;
}

template <class t_key>
storable *storable<t_key>::find( const storable<t_key> &match_me ) const
{
    storable<t_key> *current = this;
    for(; current; current = current->next )
        if( *current == match_me )                    // found a match
            return current;
}
```

The problem here is overhead. The member functions of a template class are themselves template functions. When the compiler expands out the storable template, it also expands out versions of *all* member functions of that template. Though I haven't shown them, there are probably a lot of functions defined in the storable class. Many of these functions will be like the successor() function in that they *do not use* the typing information passed to the template. That is, every expansion of this function will be identical in content to every other expansion. Of the functions that aren't like that, most of the rest will be like find, which do use the typing information, but which are easily modified not to use it.

You can solve this problem by using the template mechanism to create a derived class. Given the earlier, nontemplate implementation, you can do this:

```
template <class t_key>
class storable_tem : public storable
{
    t_key key;
public:
    virtual
    int operator==( const storable &r ) const; // Base-class override
    //...
};

template <class t_key>
/*virtual*/ int storable_tem<t_key>::operator==( const storable &r ) const
{
    t_key *right = dynamic_cast<t_key *>( &r );

    return right ? (s == r.s) : NULL;
}
```

Put another way, I have concentrated into a base class all functions that don't care what the key type is. I then use the template mechanism to create a derived-class definition that implements only those functions that need to know the key type. The net result is a considerable reduction of code size. The template mechanism can be seen as a means of automating the production of boilerplate derived classes.

Part 8.I. Exceptions

159. Intend for exceptions not to be caught.

Generally, an exception should be thrown only if:

- There's no other way to report an error (e.g. constructors, operator overloads, etc.).
- The error is unrecoverable (e.g. out of memory).
- The error is so obscure or unexpected that it won't occur to anyone to test for it (e.g. printf).

Exceptions were put into the language to handle error situations that could not otherwise be handled, such as an error that occurs in a constructor or operator-overload function. Without exceptions, the only way to detect a constructor error is to send the object a message:

```
some_obj x;
If( x.is_invalid() )
    // construction failed.
```

which is messy at best. Operator overloads present the same problem. The only way that the opera-tor+() function used in:

```
x = a + b;
```

could report an error is to return an invalid value, which would be copied to x. You could then say:

```
if( x == INVALID )
    //...
```

or some such. Again, rather messy.

Exceptions are also useful when handling errors that are usually fatal. For example, most pro-grams just call exit() if malloc() fails. All those tests like:

```
if( !(p = malloc(size)) )
    fatal_error( E_NO_MEMORY );
```

can go away if new simply doesn't return when it runs out of memory. Because new actually throws an exception [as compared to calling exit()], you can catch the exception in those rare cases where there's something you can do about the problem.

There's another issue as well. One of the reasons the ISO/ANSI C++ committee required new to throw an exception when it can't get memory is because somebody did a study and found out some ridiculous percentage of the runtime errors in real programs were caused by people not bothering to check whether malloc() returned NULL. For reasons discussed later, I don't think that an exception should be used instead of error returns just to protect programmers from themselves, but it works with new because the error is usually unrecoverable anyway. A better example might be printf(). Most C programmers don't even know that printf() returns an error code. (It returns the number of characters printed, which might be zero if the disk is full.) Programmers who do know about the error return tend to ignore it. It's not really a good idea for a program that's writing to redirected standard output to continue as if nothing were wrong, so throwing an exception might be a good idea here.

So, what's wrong with exceptions? There are really two problems. The first is readability. You'll have a hard time convincing me that:

```
some_class obj;
try
{
    obj.f();
}
catch( some_class::error &err )
{
    // do error action.
}
```

is more readable than:

```
if( obj.f() == ERROR )
    // do error action.
```

In any event, if the `try` block has more than one function call in it, you can't easily recover because you might not know where the error came from.

The following example demonstrates the the second problem. The `CFile` class, which implements basic binary file I/O, throws an exception if the disk fills during the write, as it can easily do on a floppy. Moreover, the `Write()` function doesn't return any sort of error code. An exception catch is the only way to detect an error. Here's an example of how you must detect a write error:

```
char    data[128];
CFile   f( "some_file", CFile::modeRead );

try
{
    f.Write( data, sizeof(data) );
}
catch( CFileException &r )
{
    if( r.m_cause == CFileException::diskFull )
        // do_something.
}
```

There are two problems. The first is the obvious one of the code being so ugly. I'd much rather say:

```
bytes_written = f.Write( data, sizeof(data));
if( bytes_written != sizeof(data) )
    // deal_with_it
```

The second problem is both more subtle and more serious. You can't actually recover from this error. First, you don't know how many bytes were written before the disk reached the full state. If `Write()` returned this number, you could prompt the user to swap disks, erase some nonessential files, or do something else to free up some space. You can't do that here because you don't know how much of the buffer has already been written, so you don't know where to start the write on the new disk.

Even if `Write()` did return the number of bytes written, you still couldn't recover. For example, even if `CFile` were rewritten to work as shown below, the following code wouldn't work either:

```
char     data[128];
CFile    f( "some_file", CFile::modeRead );

int bytes_written:

try
{
    bytes_written = f.Write( data, sizeof(data) );
}
catch( CFileException &r )
{
    if( r.m_cause == CFileException::diskFull )
        // do_something.

    // bytes_written contains garbage down here.
}
```

Control is transferred directly from somewhere inside `Write()` to to the `catch` block when the exception is thrown, skipping over any `return` statement inside `Write()` and also over the assignment statement in the calling function; `bytes_written` remains uninitialized. I suppose that you could pass `Write()` a pointer to a variable that it could modify to hold the number of bytes written before tossing the exception, but that's not much of an improvement. The best solution is to give up on exception tossing and return either the number of bytes written or some equivalent error indicator.

The final issue is overhead. Exception handling is very high overhead, both in times of code size and execution speed. This is the case even in operating systems like Microsoft NT, which support exception handling at the operating-system level. You can expect a 10%–20% increase in code size and a performance slow down of several percent when exceptions are used heavily.[14] Consequently, exceptions should be used only when the overhead is not an issue, an error return is usually a better choice when it's available.

160. Throw `error` objects when possible.

Listing 15 shows a simple system of class definitions used for exception tossing. I can catch read or write errors like this:

---

[14] I've measured this on the Microsoft 32-bit Visual C++ compiler; other compilers are either comparable or worse.

```
try
{
    file f("name","rw");
    buffer b;
    b = f.read()
    f.write( b );
}
catch( file::open_error &r )
{
    // File doesn't exist, can't open it.
}
catch( file::io_error &r )
{
    // some sort of unrecoverable I/O error.
}
```

If I care only that some sort of error occurred, and I don't care what sort of error, I can also do this:

```
file f;

try
{
    buffer b;
    b = f.read()
    f.write( b );
}
catch( file::error &r )
{
    //...
}
```

Listing 15. Exception Classes

```
1    class file
2    {
3    public:
4        class error                    {};
5        class open_error : public error {};
6        class io_error   : public error {};
7
8        //...
9    }
```

This code works because a `file::read_error` object *is* a `file::error` object (because it's a derived class). You can always catch a derived-class object using a base-class reference or pointer.

I could also introduce another class that used the same mechanism:

```
class long_double
{
public:
    class error                             {};
    class divide_by_zero : public error {};
    //...
};
```

Because the `error` classes are nested definitions, the names are actually `file::error` and `long_double::error`, so there's no name conflict here.

To make the maintenance easier, I always use `error` as my exception base class. (I might not use the derived classes, though, if there is only one sort of error that can happen.) This way I know that, given `some_class` that throws an exception, I can catch the exception with:

```
catch(some_class::error &r)
```

That's one less thing to look up.

When derivation is in the picture, I use the base-class `error` like this:

```
class employee
{
public:
    class error                                  {};
    class database_access_error : public error  {};
};

class peon : public employee
{
    class error : public employee::error {};
    class aagh  : public error           {};
};
```

This way an `aagh` exception can be caught as a `peon::aagh`, a `peon::error`, or an `employee::error`.

There's little point in having a global-level `error` class from which all local `error` classes derive because you can use `catch(...)` to handle this situation.

161. Throwing exceptions from constructors is tricky.

I'll preface this section with the observation that a compiler that conforms to the ANSI/ISO C++ committee's working papers won't have most of the problems discussed here. Many compilers (the Microsoft compiler is one) don't conform, however.

Errors in constructors present a real problem in C++. Because they aren't called explicitly, constructors can't return error codes in the normal way. Setting the constructed object to an "invalid" value is clunky at best and sometimes impossible. Exception tossing can provide a solution, here, but there are a lot of issues to consider. Consider the following code:

```
class c
{
    class error {};
    int *pi;
public:
    c(){ throw error(); }
    //...
};

void f( void )
{
    try
    {
        c *cp = new c;         // Cp is not initialized if the constructor
        //...                   // fails,
        delete cp;             // and this line isn't executed either.
    }
    catch( c::error &err )
    {
        printf ("Constructor failure\n");

        delete cp;            // BUG: cp holds garbage here
    }

}
```

The problem is that the memory allocated by new is never deleted. That is, the compiler allocates the memory first, then calls the constructor, which throws an error object. Control now passes directly from the constructor to the catch block. The code that assigns new's return value to cp is never executed—control jumps right over it. Consequently, there is no way to free the memory because you do not have a valid pointer. My reading of the ANSI/ISO working papers is that this behavior is incorrect—the memory should be deleted implicitly. Many compilers do it wrong, though.

Here's the easy way to fix the problem (I've put a function body in the class definition only to make the example shorter):

```
class c
{
    int *pi;
public:
    c() { /*...*/ throw this; }

};

void f( void )
{
    try
    {
        c *cp = NULL;
            cp = new c;

        c a_c_object();
    }
    catch( c *points_at_unconstructed_object )
    {
        if( !cp ) // then constructor called by 'new' failed
            delete point_at_unconstructed object;
    }
}
```

Things get tricky when some objects are allocated by new and others from the heap. You have to do something like the following to figure out what went wrong:

```
void f( void )
{
    c *cp = NULL; // Cp must be declared outside the try block because the
                  // try block forms a scope, so cp wouldn't be accessible
                  // in the catch block if it were declared in the try block.

    try
    {
        c a_c_object;
        cp = new c;
    }
    catch( c *points_at_unconstructed_object )
    {
        if( !cp ) // then constructor called by 'new' failed
            delete points_at_unconstructed_object;
    }
}
```

You can't solve this problem inside the constructor because there's no way for the constructor to know whether its initializing memory that came from new or memory that came from the stack.

In all of the previous examples, the destructor for the failed object is called even when the constructor fails and throws an exception. (It's called either indirectly by delete or implicitly when the object goes out of scope, even if it goes out of scope due to an exception toss.)

Similarly, the delete invocation indirectly calls a destructor on that object. I'll come back to this issue in a moment. Returning to the destructor issue, the failed constructor must put the object into a destroyable state before it can throw the error. Given the earlier definition for class c, the following code works only if there's no error above the new int [128] and new succeeds as well:

```
c::c( )
{
    if( some_error() )
        throw error(this);   // BUG: pi is uninitialized.
    //...
    pi = new int[128];       // BUG: pi is uninitialized if
    //...                    //      new throws an exception.
    if( some_other_error() )
    {
        delete [] pi;        // Remember to do this.
        throw error(this);   // This throw is safe.
    }
}

c::~c( )
{
    delete pi;
}
```

Remember, pi holds garbage until it's initialized from new. If the throw above the new invocation is executed or if new itself throws an exception, then pi is never initialized. (It's probably not NULL; it's uninitialized). When the destructor is called, delete is passed this garbage value. Solve the problem by initializing the pointer to a safe value before anything can go wrong:

```
c::c( ) : pi(NULL)  // initialize it in case 'new' fails
{
    if( some_error() )
        throw error(this);   // This throw is now safe.
    //...
    pi = new int[128];       // Failure of new is now safe.
    //...
    if( some_other_error() )
    {
        delete [] pi;        // Remember to delete active memory.
        throw error(this);   // This throw is safe.
    }
}

c::~c( )
{
    if( pi )
        delete pi;
}
```

You must remember to delete memory that is successfully allocated if an exception is thrown after the allocation operation, as was done previously.

You might be able to clean up the foregoing code at the user level by taking my advice from the previous rule about throwing an error object and hiding the complexity in that error object. The class definition gets much more complicated, however. The implementation in Listing 16 counts on the fact that a destructor for an explicitly declared object should be called as the try block is exited, before the catch block is executed. The destructor for an object that came from new won't be called until the memory is passed to delete, which happens in the destroy() message, sent from the catch statement. Consequently has_been_destroyed will be true only if the object didn't come from new and an exception was thrown from the constructor; it's false if the object did come from new because the destructor will not have been called yet.

Of course, you could quite reasonably argue that I've no business checking the contents of an object that has, theoretically, been destroyed. There's another problem as well. Some compilers (the Microsoft Visual C++ 2.1 compiler is one) call the destructor after the `catch` is executed, even though objects defined in the `try` block are not accessible in the `catch` block. Consequently, the code in Listing 16 won't work with these compilers. Probably the best solution would be to write a version of `operator new()` that could reliably indicate whether memory came from the heap or the stack.

Listing 16. *except.cpp*— Throwing an Exception from a Constructor

```
 1  class c
 2  {
 3  public:
 4      class error
 5      {
 6          c *p;    // NULL if successfully constructed
 7      public:
 8          error( c *p_this );
 9          void destroy( void );
10      };
11
12  private:
13
14      unsigned has_been_destroyed : 1;
15      int      *pi;
16
17  private: friend class error;
18      int been_destroyed( void );
19
20  public:
21      c() ;
22      ~c();
23
24  };
25  //==================================================================
26  c::error::error( c *p_this )
27                              : p( p_this )
28  {}
29  //------------------------------------------------------------------
30  void c::error::destroy( void )
31  {
32      if(p && !p->been_destroyed() )
33          delete p;
34  }
35  //==================================================================
36  c::c() : has_been_destroyed( 0 )
37  {
38      //...
39      throw error(this);
40      //...
41  }
42  //------------------------------------------------------------------
```

➡

Listing 16. continued...

```
43   c::~c()
44   {
45       //...
46       has_been_destroyed = 1;
47   }
48   //-------------------------------------------------------------------
49   int c::been_destroyed( void )
50   {
51       return has_been_destroyed;
52   }
53   //===================================================================
54   void main( void )
55   {
56       try
57       {
58           c *cp = new c;
59           c a_c_object;
60
61           delete cp;
62       }
63       catch( c::error &err )
64       {
65           err.destroy(); // calls destructor only if object came from new
66       }
67   }
```

Conclusion

So that's it. A lot of rules that I've found useful and that hopefully you will too. Many of the rules presented here are controversial, of course. You're welcome to argue with me about them. I certainly don't hold myself up as the Emily Post of C++ style, and I break many of these rules myself on occasion, but I honestly believe that following these rules makes me a better programmer, and I hope that you find them of some value.

I'll conclude with a question. How many C++ programmers does it take to screw in a lightbulb? None, you're still thinking procedurally. A properly designed light_bulb class would inherit a change method from a generic bulb class. Just create a derived-class object and send it a change-yourself message.

Index

About the Author

Allen Holub is a Programmer, Consultant, and Trainer specializing in C++, object-oriented design, and Microsoft operating systems. He gives inhouse training seminars throughout the U.S. and teaches for the University of California, Berkeley and Santa Cruz Extensions as well. He also works as a programmer and object-oriented-design consultant, using C and C++ in the Microsoft Windows, Windows 95, Windows NT, and UNIX environments.

Mr. Holub writes regularly for various computer magazines, including *Microsoft Systems Journal*, *Windows Tech Journal*, and occasionally *BYTE*. His popular "C Chest" column, which appeared in *Dr. Dobb's Journal* from 1983 to 1987, provided many people with their first introduction to C. His many books include *Compiler Design in C*, *C+C++*, and *The C Companion*, Mr. Holub is a composer and an instrument-rated private pilot.

You can reach him on the Internet at *allen@holub.com* or through his company, Software Engineering Consultants, P.O. Box 5679, Berkeley, CA 94702 (voice and fax: (510) 540-7954).